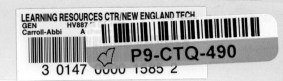

A CHANCE TO LIVE

Monsignor of the Shoe Shine Boys

A CHANCE TO LIVE

The Story of the Lost Children of the War

BY

JOHN P. CARROLL-ABBING

Translated by

CAROL DELLA CHIESA

" . . . I have found a home . . . no more blows,
misery, despair, hunger . . . only respect and a
new chance to live."

LONGMANS, GREEN AND CO.

NEW YORK · LONDON · TORONTO

1952

LONGMANS, GREEN AND CO., INC.
55 FIFTH AVENUE, NEW YORK 3

LONGMANS, GREEN AND CO., LTD.
6 & 7 CLIFFORD STREET, LONDON W 1

LONGMANS, GREEN AND CO.
215 VICTORIA STREET, TORONTO 1

A CHANCE TO LIVE

Library of Congress Catalog Card Number: 52-5917

Printed in the United States of America

FOREWORD

By His Excellency, John Lodge
Governor of Connecticut

In a generation when the lives even of men and women of large promise have been undermined by doubt and deflected by expediency, Monsignor Carroll-Abbing's works and words are a welcome and steady beacon.

To have the friendship of this gifted Irish priest, as has been my privilege, is to walk closely with greatness of spirit and mind. Even to converse with him on what to many might seem commonplace matters is an enriching experience. Goodness and light go with him.

Yet, as the reader will quickly discover, Carroll-Abbing has a deep practical understanding of human beings and their ways. Only one acutely aware of human hopes, fears, glories and backslidings could depict his fellow man with such penetrating observation.

He is an accomplished writer, this hard-working man of the cloth and one whose skill is informed with human warmth. He is a modest man, too. The reader will not learn from this book of the vast personal part played by the author in the accomplishments recounted here, or of the significant honors which have been gratefully pressed upon him.

How vivid are the pictures which he draws with a seemingly artless grace: The anarchy in Rome after Mussolini's fall, the courage and patience of the women who tramped the Umbrian hills for food for their famished children, the grisly battles in the Alban hill towns "where the sound of the spade never stopped," the trampled lawns and flowerbeds of Castel Gandolfo where, as wards of His Holiness, incredible thousands were sheltered and fed.

I found no bitterness in Carroll-Abbing's book. If there be such it is directed not against men and nations but against the ruin and misery worked by war. He writes of the German soldiers who stole away from their billets in order that he might minister to them spiritually, and who, when they saw the hunger around them, shared their rations with those whom war and disease had left wretched and hollow.

What we do find in this work is gratitude — gratitude and happiness. There is the joyful drama of his first meeting with American soldiers near Albano, and his quiet thanks for the gifts of food and clothing sent from abroad. This aid was a gift beyond price to a man who in the cruel winter of 1944–45 had seen little children livid with cold, clothed only in rough wrapping paper held together by wire.

We find him deeply grateful too that those who helped to meet the material wants of the children of Italy are now aiding him to minister to their minds and spirits. Carroll-Abbing learned what war could do to the morality of a people. He saw the enormous thieving by vagrant young boys and girls on the wharves at Naples and in other ports where the Allied armies had heaped their huge depots of food and war material. He watched on all sides a breakdown of spiritual and ethical values. Yet where other writers might have chosen to exploit sensationalism and degradation, he has instead stressed the examples of charity and brotherliness which he clearly saw shining through the threatened debacle. Where some might have vilified and condemned, he has chosen to find essential goodness and promise.

They were "like saplings," he writes, of the tough young "scugnizzi" and "sciuscia" who swarmed and thieved in the streets of the Italian cities, "saplings that had been bent by harsh winds and bitter cold, but the roots had kept strong."

Carroll-Abbing has persevered to prove that the roots indeed were strong. And today, under his loving care, — for his is a work of love — these roots, as I myself have seen, are putting out new green branches which will yet bear a fruit worthy of his inspired and patient tillage. The "Boys' Towns" of Italy and Sicily and the famous "Boys' Republic" outside Rome are monuments to his vision and energy.

You who read this book (and may your number be legion) will find, as I have found, a fitting symbolism in the fact that the now flourishing "Boys' Republic" had its start in the abandoned chambers of a battered fortress. What more apt place of beginning for one whose compassionate and luminous purpose is to fashion from the debris of war new building-stones of character, enlightenment and valid endeavor.

JOHN LODGE

Hartford, Connecticut
January 7, 1952

CONTENTS

PROLOGUE

PROLOGUE

"Who are you, who like the others have no identity
. . . who flood the world with your innocence . . .
even your evil, your unconscious evil?"

IN 1915, THE POSITION OF THE ALLIED ARMIES WITH RE-
spect to Serbia would have rendered possible a very
successful enveloping operation. It was impossible however to take full advantage of this circumstance. The
Austro-Hungarian armies, weakened by their withdrawal
from the Isonzo Front had not been able to launch their
offensive against Serbia." *

This, by now, was history.

I sat down at my desk and turned over and over in my
mind the world events of the past thirty years and the
causes that had brought them about.

The volume I had been reading was a critical analysis of
those events, as observed through the lenses of time,
gathered thoughts that had slowly matured in the minds
of men capable of considering them with detachment and
freedom from the passions of the hour.

The years between World Wars I and II had erased the
old hatreds of the first titanic struggle and nurtured new

---

* Falkenhayn: Die Oberate Heeresleitung 1914–1916 in ihren wich-
tigsten Entschliessungen-Berlin-Mittler, 1920. Page 137.

ones, new alliances, new interests in the battle of life, new means of destruction, new forms of annihilation.

As I pondered, it occurred to me how, in a few years, the events which had cut so deeply into our lives and the new bitter experiences through which we had passed would in their turn be studied, catalogued, interpreted, shelved.

The daily bulletins no longer stared at us from morning and evening papers. Gone were the war words flashed from the radio to anxious listeners. We had only facts now, cold figures, international agreements, political conferences. . . .

A never-ending stream of values, documents, names followed one upon the other, date succeeding date, the whole bringing about a confusion of thought that even tomorrow might serve to divide nations and unleash the fury of another and more brutal conflict.

Thus would World War II also pass into history to be cogitated over by student and scientist alike, and by us who, in the perusal of endless volumes born of the War, might not even remember how we, too, had lived in that orgy of blood and horror.

The Maginot Line, Dunkirk, Coventry, Tobruk, Anzio, Cassino, the Gothic Line, Okinawa, the Pacific, Hiroshima, all of them will be only names, I figured, associated no doubt with the many words that had been newly coined in technical phraseology.

Encirclement, scorched earth, partisans, these must be defined and written down for posterity to study and understand.

The true sense of their meaning would be forgotten. Few

would reflect as they read them upon the passionate human elements hidden within. Few would realize the fact that an order given for the prevention of certain moves on the Mediterranean Front might have caused the death of thousands of human beings, that because of that general's initiative other thousands lay dead or wounded on a far-flung battlefield or that countless villages peopled mostly by the very young or the very old had been completely wiped out.

I dreamed on. The years between '39 and '45, crowded, living years rose before me. I saw never-ending lines of young unknown boys and mature men, ghosts of the past, of the immediate past. They had died in every corner of the earth, in every clime, from the margins of the Poles to the jungles of the Equator, in the waters of the Pacific and the Atlantic, on the fields of France, in Russia, in Japan, in China. Other faces were smiling and gay. Happy faces of bright lads whose names rose in my mind as I gazed at them — Pasquale, Jackie, Gennaro, Hans. Here they were in that silent sea of ghostly faces, ghosts of the once living, breathing boys I had known . . . now no longer with us.

The sea of faces dimmed and others appeared. I recognized Toni, Joe, Charlie. They looked at me with sad eyes, eyes that were still large and expressive, wide with suffering, as they had been, when gazing at me from their hospital beds. Where are you all now? Where are you, Carlo, with your arms cut clean at the elbow? Remember how hard you tried to smile to cheer up your old dad? How you succeeded in hiding your black thoughts from him?

The sky darkened. The youths of twenty and twenty-five, the mature men passed on, and their places were taken by others, mere boys in their teens now and little children who still spoke shyly. Jimmy, Franco, Bobbie, Teresa, children with no eyes, no arms, no legs. Orphans who in the fury of war had lost all the tender care of their young years. No one walked with these as they wept for the home destroyed, the fireless hearth, the child's thirst for love.

The procession moved on. Barefoot boys and girls, hungry tots, ragged, faces caked with the unwashed dirt and grime of months, hopeless with the misery of lonely children. Who are you, who like the others have no identity, who like them flood the world with your innocence, your simplicity, even your evil, your unconscious evil? Is Enzo there who in a hospital ward smiled his last smile as I passed? Or Michael who succeeded after all in reaching the African coast where he had been born? And Beppe who fell under the wheels of the monster tank?

Mourning, pain, death in the procession, in the endless procession. Curly heads, sleek ones, fair golden ones and dark, thin scrawny bodies barely covered by strips of rags. Along with these small beings who wandered aimlessly and hopelessly the streets of a dark city, town, or hamlet stalked the living proof of what hate can and does do.

I

SUFFERING SCHOOL OF LOVE

I

SUFFERING SCHOOL OF LOVE

"Remember always that God is near and He will be
your strength in time of need"

THE DAY OF THE ITALIAN ARMISTICE MARKED THE BE-
ginning of a new way of life for the Romans. Everything had fallen apart as it were. Any form of organization
had disappeared; morale was at its lowest. They thought
of themselves as a lost people. Face to face with God and
their own consciences, many individuals sought to awaken
a degree of personal initiative, but with all central authority gone, a day soon dawned when anarchy was ready to
lift its ugly head.

The need for peace and tranquillity was imperative, but
how was it to be achieved? I saw strong men weep like children as they spoke to me of their men dispersed, their
homes destroyed, their country prostrate and helpless.
They longed for escape from everything and came to me
begging for a corner in which to live alone, far from the
all-encircling, stalking horror.

In the Hospital of the Knights of Malta where I was
stationed, we needed more and more workers. Here at
least a number found a haven of safety from the danger
of being drafted for the armies fighting in the North or
of being sent to the concentration camps of Germany.

Hour by hour, day by day, the tension grew. The fear of

9

some sudden German move was in every heart, but the work at the hospital went on as usual.

Refugees from the northern provinces came drifting in. For a time they stayed in Rome, hidden away in attics and cellars. Then, as the opportunity offered itself, they crossed the German lines and sought refuge in the South.

One incident came to my attention, which in its simple significance needs no explanation. How often a shading in the forming of a judgment can cause useless misunderstanding!

On a Roman street a gaunt red-haired youth nervously paces before the door of a church. He keeps at it for all of an hour. Finally he turns and enters the dark interior after glancing suspiciously up and down the street.

A short time goes by and he emerges accompanied by a white-haired priest. The two walk in silence along the narrow streets, purposely avoiding the busier thoroughfares. They reach one of the poorer sections of the city. No marble palaces here, no blossoming gardens, only a dense mass of starving humanity.

The priest and his tall companion halt a moment before a modest home and then climb the steps.

Their story was told to me some time later. The man was an English prisoner of war who had made his escape from a German concentration camp in Italy. Some weeks earlier, the old priest had been able to hide him, by making arrangements for him to live with a family that had been willing to give him the care and protection he needed. He had been given a room, a fairly good bed in it; he was allowed to listen to the radio and follow the news of the advancing Allies. The food was not too abundant, but he could not complain. No one was eating much those days.

"They treat me well enough, Father," he had said by way of explanation of his sudden visit that afternoon, "but I wish they would stop being so hard to talk to. They never say a word to me, beyond a short greeting. Why can't I be given a friendly smile once in a while? Why don't they ask me to share their meals with them at their own table, instead of letting me eat by myself day after day? Why can't I go into their sitting room? Am I poison? They may be good to me in their way, Father, but to tell you the truth, I think all they are interested in is the few pennies I bring them . . . I'm fed up with it, I tell you."

The priest listened patiently and accompanied him back to the house.

"It's this way, Father," the woman of the house said almost apologetically. "There are four of us in the family, he makes five. You know how hard it is to get food these days and yet my husband, my two children, and the captain must be fed. I spend hours and hours in my search for bare necessities. Yesterday I found some rice and two eggs. The captain ate the eggs and the rice, my children had only the rice. How can we let him see how things are? He is our guest . . . he is far away from home. At least we are together . . . we did not want to embarrass him."

A little time later the priest left the house. There was a look of satisfaction on his face.

The Englishman and the Italians remembered the word enemy only as a word after that. A brighter comprehension of the true meaning of life, far above mere boundaries or contrasting ideologies and interests, replaced the misunderstanding of the days that had gone by . . . forever.

Episodes such as this revealed the basic goodness of man, true charity offered without a thought of self or of selfish aims. And I marveled then, as I was to continue to marvel in the future, how it was the very poor, those whose sufferings had been greatest, that showed the most sublime spirit of Christian charity. It has been well said that in the school of suffering the lesson of love is always taught and often learned.

Several months later, during the retreat of the German Army from the capital, another incident was brought to my attention.

A number of German soldiers were going through the San Giovanni Gate. Some of them, exhausted and spent, threw themselves on the ground for a moment's respite. They crouched, silent and brooding, under the arches of the Basilica, and waited.

The Italian women of the nearby buildings led by pure compassion went in and out of their homes to give them food and water, in complete forgetfulness of the oppression that still lived in their hearts and in their flesh for the anguish and the terrors of the occupation.

Some might call this weakness. To others this simple act speaks of the real greatness of the Italian soul. I compared these women to Veronica who took pity on Our Lord as He climbed to Calvary.

But hate was still alive. It continued to spread its terror upon the helpless city. The raids, the arrests, the deportations tore children from their mothers, husbands from their wives. Rumors of unspeakable cruelties were frequent and most of them true.

The news of the Fosse Ardeatine massacre froze all hearts with its horror, a horror that destroyed all my hopes of saving many lives I had fought for so long.

My own sorrow would have been much greater if I had known that among the victims was a certain Lieutenant Giglio. Tall, blond, only twenty-one years of age when I first met him, I have remembered him through the years for his honesty, his simplicity, the childlike loyalty of his great soul. He had left the hospital after a few months and I had never seen him again.

He had escaped to the southern end of the Peninsula and then had returned to Rome, sent there by the Allied Command on a secret mission. He was betrayed and tortured with the most refined of cruelties together with his faithful attendant in a Roman "pension" which in subsequent days became abjectly famous.

Weakened by torture, his body reduced to a bloody mass by scourgings and beatings, but proud to the end, taking upon himself all responsibility for his actions, he had not betrayed any of his companions. He died a hero.

Lieutenant Giglio's moral stature had risen to great heights in two short years. The hardships he had endured had only strengthened his spirit.

In the account written by his faithful attendant and friend, no one can fail to be deeply moved by the simple narrative:

"The lieutenant found the strength to lift a cup of water to my lips and hand me a piece of bread . . . he blamed himself alone and often said to me: 'Poor Scotti . . . all because of me . . .'

"His captors brought the man who had betrayed him to his cell. When the latter tried to deceive him with protestations of friendship, he did not even bother to answer him. He just said as he went out: 'Walter, you are another Judas . . .'

"At the Fosse he encouraged others . . ."

In 1947 his mother came to see me. She had become interested in a small boy she had found in the street, an orphan. Her eyes filled as she greeted me. Seeing me reminded her of her son.

"I'm sorry, Father. I thought I was stronger . . ."

Her words sounded an echo in my heart, as she handed me a book which I had given her son and in which I had written these words in dedication to him:

"Remember always that God is near and He will be your strength."

Strange, paradoxical and often humorous incidents arose in that ever-changing conglomeration of people who sought refuge in the capital or who came to see me at the hospital for diverse reasons.

Two visitors came to see me one morning. They were both tall, fair, with healthy looks and a certain air of carefree good humor about them. We spoke at length in my office. On our way out of the hospital, one of the orderlies called me back.

"Monsignor, I wouldn't go with those two, if I were you," he whispered mysteriously in my ear. "You can see a mile away they are guards in disguise."

He was sincere and anxious. I laughed heartily and assured him everything was all right. They happened to be two priests from Ireland. Their very blond looks had been enough to brand them as suspicious characters.

The Romans with their mordant wit and their habit of ridiculing everything and everybody often proved that even under the stress of the moment they had not lost their inborn feeling that time in one way or another solves all problems. It was the lesson of centuries of struggle being once again put to the test.

Below the walls of Castel Sant'Angelo, where the magnificent bridge leads to the Mole Adriana, a German sentinel stood rigid and ungainly in his ill-fitting uniform. Now and again he took a few steps, trying hard to get the stiffness out of his legs.

The air of the Tiber blew cold and damp. It was about four o'clock in the afternoon. Rose-tinted clouds moved slowly across the intense blue of the sky in one of those unforgettable Roman sunsets.

Two men came sauntering down the length of the bridge chanting and gesticulating. On reaching the spot where the sentinel stood, they halted. He looked them over suspiciously. They returned his stare and then leaned over to read the inscription at the foot of a group of statues that stands at the entrance to the bridge.

"Have you seen this inscription?" one of them asked turning innocently to the frowning guard. "No? Well, let me read it to you. Listen. It says, that many years ago, a French soldier stood on the very spot on which you are standing now . . . understand?" He added no other comment, but a sly smile hovered on his lips as he strolled off with his friend.

The German gazed after them, a puzzled look on his face. The walls of the ancient castle frowned down upon him, the Tiber continued its ebb and flow against the old pillars of the bridge, as it had done century after century.

The women showed a greater degree of self-control than the men under the pressure of circumstances. They grumbled a lot, but the love of their children sustained them, while they walked miles of dusty roads in search of food, often only grass or roots for the daily meal. We saw long lines waiting hours for a draught of milk, well-watered most of the time, or for a bit of coal, damp, crumbling at the least touch and insufficient for their needs.

On those slowly moving lines, the maid and the mistress, the washwoman and the schoolteacher talked and exchanged opinions, impressions, the various means of procuring the much-needed something for the ones waiting patiently at home. Long trips had to be made, at times as far as the Umbrian hills, that the children might not suffer too much.

And while the mothers searched and waited in line, the fathers fought in battle, languished in concentration camps, hid in caves and in cellars, died.

The children lived an unnatural existence, far removed from that of years gone by, when, from their very cradles, they had had such tender care. The home and its control vanished and the youngsters enjoyed a limitless freedom, an easy independence that was soon to have dire consequences.

One small boy, with dark, bright, intelligent eyes, was brought to the hospital late at night. His trousers in shreds showed his legs cut and bleeding from the all-too-evident shrapnel wounds. No complaint came from his lips. To the contrary, he told of his deeds with the air of a man of the world, accustomed to battle and the risks it involved.

After the curfew he had been on his way to deliver a message to a relative hiding in some corner of the city. On the return trip, he had been stopped for questioning by the German patrol. The questions were far from his liking and he had made a dash for freedom. The hand grenade fell short, but a number of fragments had found their mark in the boy's body.

I talked to him as he lay on the operating table, trying to keep his mind from the ordeal. The doctor was busy and the little patient continued to chatter and joke.

"That was a big one, eh, doctor . . . it took a long time to dig that one out. . . ."

He was proud of his prowess and richly embroidered the true facts. He was all of twelve . . . he spoke like an old man.

The heavy German uniforms, the slow movements of the wearers gave the swift-footed youngsters of the streets a good advantage. Giovanni and Mario and Giacomo tormented their unwelcome hosts in every conceivable and often inconceivable way. They poked fun at them, laughed at them, tricked them and usually came out the victors.

A group of them would hide behind a door watching and waiting while another was being questioned, while arguments rose and fell. The arguments at their height, the second group went to work. A call, innocent enough, the whistling of a few bars of a significant and perhaps compromising tune, and more boys appeared, two, five, ten. An indolent air, a wink, a hand deep in pocket, a hunched shoulder, a goose step, then a word said in apparent jest, yet subtle, drew the attention of the patrol. Off went the first group, the second strolling on, starting a game or standing about, a friendly silly grin on each mischievous face.

The Germans raged and fumed, but there was little they could do. Luckily for Rome, the child population was numerous and it soon turned out to be the main problem of the occupying army. For their friends, the youngsters were invaluable, for under what might be called an outer mask, an ever-growing army of men of all social distinctions slowly wove a thick net of messages and counter-messages, at the same time eking out a miserable existence in broken ruins, in walled-up rooms, ready at a moment's notice to shed their blood in defense of an ideal, or for the safety of a friend. The children kept communications open.

In the period between September of 1943 and June of

1944, the walls of Rome showed up again and again covered with crudely painted signs in brilliant crimson. Their meaning was obvious and shook the fraying nerves of the Germans. The signs praised liberty and peace, equality of races, and everyone knew that many of them had been made by the small members of the Roman population.

Unmindful of danger, used to it by this time, they went about at night, small dark shadows lost in the blackout, and accomplished their jobs swiftly and efficiently, armed with a pail, a brush, and a wonderful exhilarating feeling inside.

Most of the signs appeared in the more humble sections of the city, where the criss-crossing streets offered many avenues of escape. One night, in the ancient Trastevere section of Rome, two boys had started their task on the walls of an old palace. They had gone to work shortly before midnight. The alleys were deserted and they thought themselves safe. Unluckily for them, two S.S. patrols suddenly emerged from opposite corners. Trapped between two fires, they did their best to escape. In the confusion they dashed down a blind alley. The next morning they were discovered bleeding and unconscious. One of them died the next day, the other was left a hopeless cripple.

Much has been said in evaluating the fine behavior of these boys in their struggle for freedom. Discussions have grown lengthy about whether to attribute it to heroism or to a momentary exaltation of the spirit. For myself, it is sufficient for me to recall the innumerable instances of self-control I witnessed, the proud consciousness of self, the spirit of independence, of social solidarity, of sacrifice for an ideal. I do not ask myself why.

One Sunday morning the news invaded the capital that the Allies had landed at Anzio.

The weather had been so mild and sunny, I had made plans for taking a group of my convalescents out for a picnic on the hills of Monte Mario. They needed a change. As we set out, one of the doctors tried to dissuade me, especially since we would have to cross the Tiber to get to our destination and it was feared the Germans might blow up the bridges in their retreat and leave us stranded.

I was against disappointing my men and we started.

"After all," I told them, "if we are cut off, we can let you have news of ourselves by way of the Vatican Radio."

I must admit that, as we went along, I had an unpleasant feeling of apprehension. What if we really were cut off? What would happen?

Lunch over, I decided to shorten the trip. We turned toward Rome, and hastened back to the city. A bus was to take us on the last leg of the journey. At the corner where the bus was supposed to stop, we found a carabinier looking rather dazed and bewildered.

"I don't think the bus will come," he said to us. "I think the Americans are in Rome."

His words did not seem too strange as all this time a never-ending line of German cars, trucks, and ambulances loaded with wounded was passing us on the road and heading for the North. They had all the appearance of an army in retreat.

We had no alternative. We waited. At the bridge, the sentinels, more rigid than ever, demanded a stricter obedience of orders. Several camouflaged tanks passed us hurrying in the opposite direction.

We found the hospital pervaded by an air of excitement. That evening we climbed the stairs to the roof. From there we could look toward Anzio and watch for the Allied advance.

Rome stretched out below us, murky, sooty. To the right the immense dome of Michelangelo, before us the crowded streets of the Trastevere. In the distance the white marble pile of the Victor Emmanuel II monument rose out of the surrounding shadows.

Nothing happened that night, nothing for many nights to come. Our waiting hopeless, the stairs became steeper and steeper, our hearts leaden. Even the panorama had turned commonplace. Soon we abandoned our evening vigil.

Throughout the centuries the Romans have had a deep-seated feeling of security engendered no doubt by the presence of the Holy Father. In this conflict also, most of the people placed their hopes in him for the safety and final liberation of Rome.

Many, however, entertained an apprehensive fear that more suffering would come and they prepared themselves to meet the future in a material as well as a spiritual way.

"There is no escape. Rome will be another Stalingrad."

In the meantime war raged in unrestrained fury in the zone known as "Castelli Romani." Also known as the

Albani Mountains, they form a natural barrier to the east of Anzio encircling Rome as a ring of strongholds, separating it from the wide plains that roll out to the sea.

The Allied troops waged their fiercest battles against these hills where the Germans had entrenched themselves. Thus the Castelli became the favorite target of the Allied bombardiers, since they formed the rearguard of the German lines.

Genzano, Velletri, Castel, Gandolfo, Albani were the tortured towns of those regions where Nature had been so prodigal in her gifts of beauty and peace.

Immediately after the Anzio landing, I had my first experience with actual warfare.

The proximity of the battlefield to the Castelli and the continuous air skirmishes had made imperative the evacuation of all the childrens' institutes in the area and I had gone myself to organize their transfer to the capital.

I had just reached Albano under a lowering sky, when against the clouds in the distance I spied a formation of heavy bombers speeding toward us. We were walking along the principal street. In a few moments the bombers passed over us, the rumble of their motors now loud, now cut almost to a murmur, while the inhabitants merely gazed at them from window or door. Flat against the sky the compact mass moved on toward Rome and was lost in the gray.

Life in the little town continued as before. A woman went on washing her clothes before her doorstep, children played in the square, the sound of a blacksmith's hammer struck its rhythmic beat.

A few moments and pandemonium broke loose. Another squadron of planes had made its appearance. The same curiosity, the same indifference, the same eyes turned to the sky. The woman stopped a moment in her washing, a baby garment in her upheld hand, the hammer beat on.

The holding of breath, an instant of waiting, a cry, a shout from a dozen throats, a hundred, then a mad dash for safety. A bomb, another and yet another dropped on the village, burst with a deafening roar, earsplitting, shaking the earth under us.

I dashed into a store seeking protection from the flying shrapnel. The owner of the store drew me swiftly toward the rear.

Hardly had we stepped into the room when I had the impression that everything about us was disintegrating. Chunks of mortar fell from the ceiling, the room swayed and we were thrown against the back wall. Then walls and ceiling gradually gave way entirely.

I was stunned, white with the shock and the plaster, but I was still alive. My friend, the storekeeper, was moaning not far from me. Together we managed to dig ourselves out, climbed over the rubble and found an opening into the street. It was deserted.

Cries and moans came from a house struck in full by the rain of bombs. Clouds of dust, dry throats, coated tongues, choked nostrils . . . we breathed with difficulty. In the far heavens the rumble of the planes.

This was not my first experience of an air raid. I had been under the bombs in many towns, but it was the first time I had felt death so close. And for days the terror continued. Twice the buildings that sheltered me were struck and partly demolished. Somehow I escaped. And without so much as a scratch.

I knew the Castelli well. I had been there often in happier days. It was pleasant to remember the varied green of the trees mottled by the rich brown of the well-tilled field, the long lines of silver vineyards, the giant cypresses that rose unexpectedly in the distance against the blue, the festive air of the crowded villages and hamlets, busy at marketing their wines or their grapes, white, blue, red, black, still touched with the morning dew. I recalled the small blue trams scuttling from village to village in clattering haste. Life, gay, untrammeled, unhurried, an almost patriarchal existence, far from the rush and the bustle of the capital. I shall never forget the profusion of children in the streets, running, shouting, restless, happy, the cup of their joy brimming over as the cup of sparkling wine offered to the visitor. Where was it all now?

A few days later I was asked to go out to the Castelli again to accompany several ambulances that were to pick up a number of wounded and take them to Rome. The ambulances were ready to start on their return journey when a man dashed up to me, his face distorted with anguish. In broken words he begged me to go with him. A two-year-old child was in serious condition and was in need of an immediate operation. Only in Rome could he be saved.

I told the driver to wait and followed the man. He led me through the village and by numerous byways to the region around Lake Nemi. Night had come by this time. Not a

G. I. Handout

These were the street boys

A first glimpse of Boys' Town

His first real bed

The start of a new day

light showed in the vast darkness. The waters of the lake held a vague fluorescent gleam, the somber shadows of trees and hill outlined its gloom. It was hard to see the way.

My guide finally took a narrow, barely practicable path and I followed as best I could. Up and down and up again, along a dykelike formation until he came to a stop before an opening in the ground. With a brief nod he went in. I found myself in a deep tunnel.

For a moment or two I could make out absolutely nothing. We were in comparative darkness. I stumbled along, then, as my eyes grew accustomed to the blackness, I distinguished dim outlines by the faint lights in the wall of the tunnel. Tiny candles. The path I was treading was a sort of gallery, low, damp. In a single long row, men, women and children huddled, lay, sat, sick with fear, hungry, minds and bodies dulled by the fetid air, by the absence of sunlight. It was a story from the pen of Poe. These were living ghosts from the imagination of a Doré.

The man ahead of me had never stopped in his hurried advance and I had managed to keep up with him. The line of breathing skeletons never seemed to end. I learned that more than three thousand people had taken refuge there.

An undescribable foulness rose from that multitude of beings.

In this ghastly horror men lived, men who had spent their lives in the sun. Children huddled who had danced on the hills. Eyes that had been sparkling with life were now spent, lips had lost their smiles, cheeks their color.

For a whole month many had been unable to leave the tunnel. The sick and the old lay as if shelved, on wicker gratings hanging from the ceiling.

For almost a mile the nightmare continued. The sick child was lying on an old coat. The faint light from a candle etched deep shadows on the sunken cheeks, his eyes bright with fever were wide open, suffering and fright filling their depths. Close to him crouched another child, the same sunken cheeks, the same fear.

I lifted the small figure in my arms and returned to the hole in the ground, followed by the prayers of the entombed.

"Pray for us, Father, that all this may soon be over," they pleaded.

I breathed the cool air and as I held the little one, my thoughts strayed to the hundreds of other tunnels . . . caves . . . holes, where thousands upon thousands of human beings had turned into moles. . . . War!

That crowd of human beings, creatures of God, persecuted, tortured by misfortune never left my mind in the days to come. It would be impossible even for the most hardened mind to forget the horrific vision I had witnessed.

Some way had to be found, even within the limits of present conditions, of assuaging the unbearable tortures of these innocent people.

Genzano following the bombardment of February 12, 1944, had been almost completely destroyed and while a thousand or so of its inhabitants continued to live in its ruins, the others, close to eight thousand, had burrowed in caves.

Albano, another town, had been completely evacuated under order of the German Command. Part of its inhabitants had been sheltered in the papal villa at Castel Gandolfo, the others repeated the story . . . caves . . . around Lake Albano this time.

Velletri also had not been spared. Its inhabitants scattered through the hills, directly in the path of the battling armies. These were probably the most unfortunate, for added to the absolute lack of food and adequate shelter they often found themselves under direct artillery fire.

The civil authorities of the zone established its offices in Rome when the Castelli were declared evacuated. The fact that tens of thousands of poor people still lived in the area was officially ignored. They had to shift for themselves, abandoned, completely isolated.

Few doctors could be found in those miles of regions, but the few, it can be stated without fear of exaggeration, faced the situation with heroism and indefatigable devotion.

During the first week, I saw one of these men operate amidst the most unbelievable squalor. There was no way of getting the patient to a hospital, the operation was not difficult, but it was urgent. On a mattress far from sterile, bare of covering, lay a man still young in years. The only light in the room came from five candles held high by three women. The murky darkness was barely split by the faint glow. In shirt sleeves the doctor cut, his hand steady.

Silence weighed on the scene in the cave, in contrast to the cannon fire outside. I heard the soft sobbing of a woman, the rasping cough of two old men. The steam rising from the pot of water at the end of the table mingled with the black smoke rising from the candles and increased the surgeon's difficulties.

"I should have been shot for operating under those conditions," he said to me as he finished. He had taken a big chance, and in taking it he had only done what he felt was his duty.

The problems facing us were many and the solution not a simple one. Everything was needed and we had nothing to give, no food to distribute, no medicine, no clothing. Besides all this, the zone was a military one. All means of communications had been interrupted or destroyed. The situation was enough to discourage even the most stouthearted.

What was to be done? Where was I to begin?

I decided to limit my activities for the present to the organization of medical relief.

In the caves crowds waited and watched. They feared the spread of an epidemic and realized their inability to fight it. A great number had already died, the very old and the very young, the sick, the wounded struck down during the air raids. A little care, a small supply of medicine, some indispensable drugs and they might have been saved.

Friends and acquaintances, informed of my purpose, began to send me some of the money I so much needed. With it I was able to buy a great quantity of disinfectants and thus provide for the disinfecting of the grottoes and shelters, where the greatest danger lurked. Furthermore, my shelves began to boast of the much-wanted sulfa drugs, bandages, gauze and other first-aid necessities.

One of my friends showed a certain degree of surprise when I went to him for help.

"I thought that for you priests, charity was only a means for reaching the soul," he said to me.

"You are right in a way," I countered, "it would be wrong for us not to think primarily of the soul, but charity of a material nature has its great value also. It is up to us to see that suffering is relieved."

He smiled in a knowing way.

"But are you not always preaching that the good things of this earth have little worth, that we must resign ourselves to our sufferings?"

"Resign ourselves to our own sufferings yes, in order not to waste their value. But we cannot resign ourselves to the sufferings of others, nor should we forget that there is a certain value to the good things of this world. They are, after all, the means by which we reach our final destiny. Very often, it is true, we allow them to become obstacles in our path. You can see that for yourself. The man who is deeply attached to the riches and honors of this world has hardly the time and the desire for a close relationship with other people's troubles. He fears too much the loss of his wealth and power. It is those who have little who are lavish with their time and their money."

"Suffering, school of love . . . have I not heard that before?" concluded my friend and reached for his wallet.

I looked at him with a smile.

"You blackguard! You have made me waste my time talking to you."

Another problem I had to solve was how to provide for the transportation to Rome of the seriously wounded cases. I appealed to the director of the hospital, explained the whole situation to him and without any further ado, I begged him for ambulances from the Military Order of Malta, these to be used exclusively in the Castelli area, but, probably through an oversight, no prohibition explicitly mentioned the Order of Malta or the Ministry of Public Health. The German authorities had given the order that no ambulances of the Italian Red Cross were to leave the capital. It was my plan to take advantage of this to set up a first-aid service. Cardinal Canali, in charge of the civil administration of the Vatican City State, authorized me to draw on their small gasoline reserve for this purpose.

As soon as news of this new organization began to spread, a score of teen-agers offered their services to me. They collaborated splendidly with me even from the start. Our efforts gave rise to the Medical Assistance Corps for the stricken areas of the Castelli Romani. In future months it was extended to include the Frosinone and Cassino zones and then it became known as the War Zones Medical Corps.

On set days we started out at an early hour with our ambulances. We made our rounds of the hill towns, picking up the wounded and the sick, and leaving in our medical centers the supplies we had bought.

Once the ambulances had been filled, they returned to Rome, leaving us in whatever village we had chosen as our starting point for the week. There was so much to be done and we needed more and more help, but in a few weeks we were able to see some improvemnt.

We walked hundreds of miles along country roads and pathways strafed by machine-gun fire and aerial bombardments in search of patients, scattered and hidden in the hills, in hundreds of caves and burrows. Everywhere we found the same misery, thousands of starving sick people.

The boys who worked with me were tireless in their forgetfulness of self, serene and enthusiastic. They worked with no personal interest involved, no selfish wish for self-aggrandizement. They were ever the first to rush in, helping the stricken under the rain of death from the sky, seeking lost children. Thousands of cubic feet of caves were made safe through them.

Their sense of humor never failed them even in the most trying circumstances. As we returned from one of our excursions, the cannon suddenly boomed. We sought safety in a sort of trench in the bend of a hill. There we waited for the battle to end. Two of the boys began a discussion . . . of all things on men's fashions! One poked fun at another. The cannon boomed louder. I wondered if they could be deaf.

"Boys, where do you think you are? In a café? Don't you know what's going on?" I called to them.

They burst out laughing and shot back to realities.

The will to do more, the will to do everything, to multiply our efforts, drove us on and on. Each man had to do the work of ten, of a score.

One feat accomplished, a dozen others awaited us. Medical centers were founded, food was distributed, lost children were gathered in, isolated centers were brought back into the living world.

The ambulance was a symbol of life. It came to mean assurance of aid, moral comfort, a sense of not having been forgotten, the certainty of no longer being alone.

News again spread from village to village. A few miles only had separated them, but it might have been thousands.

"Do you mean to tell us there are others living like this?" they asked, unbelieving.

The same broken families, the same equality of misery, each small world a sea of tragedy, each small community suffering the same misfortune but judged as the worst, as the most urgent, when in reality they were all identical from the psychological and material point of view.

There were times when I had to go alone into enemy camps in order to reach my destinations. As I passed, a questioning look lurked in the eyes of the German soldiers.

"What does he think he is doing here?"

It was not difficult to read the meaning of those glances.

Sometimes the Czechs and the Poles dropped into my cave to speak to me. They had been forcibly conscripted into the German Army and now found themselves among men with whom they had little in common. Their traditions, their education, their language were unlike those of the Germans. They looked to me for a word of understanding. They shared with me their thoughts and their worries, they recounted the tales of the tragedy of their lives. I heard of their wives, their children, of their longing to see them.

"No, Father, I don't want to die . . . my old woman is still waiting for me. . . ."

Now and then the Germans opened their hearts to me.

In the beginning when we had to go through the German lines, we met some opposition. As the days passed, we began to be recognized and our relations improved. Although cold and distant, at least they treated us courteously. From words I heard and actions I witnessed, I saw their own tension growing.

One day I had to call on a local German commander to protest against certain incidents that had taken place. He was self-controlled and coldly proud. He promised to look into the matter. I made some other remark. Suddenly he stood up and beat his fist on the table before him.

"Seven years, seven whole years! Good God, how long?"

They were beginning to break under the strain of this interminable war.

On the Anzio front thousands died.

In a field kitchen a soldier struck off the names of entire battalions.

At Eastertime some of them crept furtively in a forest of bare blackened trunks, where the luxurious vegatation had all been destroyed. No one was to know they had come in search of the comfort only God could dispense. They received Him humbly in Holy Communion. A few miles distant the roar and the boom and the crash continued.

Rows and rows of bodies awaited burial on those once verdant hills . . . the sound of the spade never stopped . . . and then row upon row of new graves. The shattered broken bodies had found rest.

Pity choked my throat, contracted my heart. I gazed at the dead faces of those eighteen-year-olds and I wondered if among them I might not see some of the boys I had known and joked with in the Germany of what seemed so long ago, in the peaceful southern Germany I had so much enjoyed.

I stopped near a gravedigger to bless the dead, to say a prayer for them and their loved ones. Sharp words from the digger, dark looks of hate from another. I gave a final blessing and left. . . .

I remember that period of my life as a horrible nightmare.

There was little time to think, yet the thought that I was not to come out alive from that inferno of hate and suspicion persisted.

Near one of the small towns lived an old couple. In their tiny hut they relied on the food we brought them to eke out their lonely existence.

One night as I was on my way to them, the dark sky suddenly burst into flame . . . another battle. . . .

I took refuge in a cave. Time passed and the battle went on. My situation was not a happy one. All I could do was wait and hope.

I tried to pray . . . my mind kept wandering. The solitude became oppressive.

I reached my old friends' home at a very late hour. They

thanked me for what I had brought. There had been nothing for them to eat that day.

After they had eaten, they asked me to hear their confession.

"Strange, Father," the woman said to me as I bid goodbye to them, "before this war we had everything we wanted, a vineyard, two cows, vegetables, chickens. We lacked nothing and yet God seemed very far away. The church was near enough, but my husband never went there and I . . . well, you know how it is, Father . . . to tell the truth we had not prayed as we should for years. We weren't bad, but there is so much to be done on a farm. And now God has taken away all we had and He seems so near. It's as if He had done this so we could find Him again. The whole world is full of Him. . . ."

They took me to the door and I left them in their solitude. Solitude? Far from it. That was not solitude. On my return trip I, also, no longer felt alone. The presence of God was very real.

Night often found me and my boys in the most out of the way places. During those five months we slept in tumbledown huts, in cellars, in stables. We knew laughter as well as hardships, as the night when a lonely goat came to nuzzle at our faces and a piglet grunted for hours in its sty, asking for company.

Frequently we spent the night in the Salesian building that only a short time before had been a flourishing Institute.

In agreement with the superior who had been enthusiastic about my plans, I had organized it as a small hospital, a haven for many homeless refugees. It was impossible for the ambulances at our disposal to transport all the sick and wounded to Rome. Here the less dangerously wounded found shelter. The gymnasium was well suited to this purpose. My young helpers had done wonders in a short time in putting everything in good working order.

Three Salesian brothers did the best they could under the direction of a young priest whose face looked even younger than his years. His great sense of humor relieved the tension of the moment, giving us the opportunity of a good laugh and a hearty joke. Possessed with the qualities of real charity, he fulfilled the ideal of the great founder of his order, Saint John Bosco. This was the first time I had come in contact with the Salesians and I realized then to what heights they had raised this idea, in the love they showered on their unfortunate brethren.

Our apartment, if I may call it that, was in one of the cellars of the old Institute. It was murky with smoke, the air foul from the sheep grease of the candles we burned. In the vague light the cellar assumed a Gothic look, aided by the heavy wooden posts, wedged between the floor and the ceiling to fortify the roof during aerial attacks.

A number of old men shared the place with us. In the rear, separated by a partition, a nucleus of German officers had their quarters. Often during the night they awakened us with songs and the sporadic sound of shots.

Near my bed behind a small curtain I had erected a small altar. We said Mass there in the morning. Whenever I could not sleep, a faint glow told me I was not alone. It came from the tiny vigil light burning before the Blessed

Sacrament. I watched with Him. That glow, lost in the darkness of that cellar, grew into a great burning fire, a driving force for the work of the morrow, a sign of faith and hope, love and encouragement.

At eventide, if things permitted it, we gathered together in a small corner. A table and a few chairs filled the whole space. The candlelight deepened the proportions of the room, the corners were lost in gloom.

We chatted, discussed, questions and answers rose spontaneously, we even found cause for a joke or a laugh. Serenity and a feeling of peace refreshed our fagging minds, relaxed our tired muscles. For a few moments at least the horror was forgotten.

The moments seldom lasted. A word hung suspended . . . eyes looked into eyes . . . we listened. Noise in the distance . . . detonations . . . the Germans had begun another attack.

Up we climbed to the terrace to watch the spectacle. Flares streaked the sky. I was reminded of a village feast in honor of the patron saint. Rigid near us, the Germans also stood and kept watch. In each heart a sensation, in each a reaction, under an open sky, helpless.

Below us, scattered in the green hills, hidden in the crumbling ruins, the tired thousands prayed for surcease and one more chance to live, to dream of country, home, family, mutual love and devotion, longing for the lost fireside, the lost caresses of a mother no longer there.

We left the terrace . . . a bomb had struck a nearby target . . . we had more work to do. . . .

The great sufferers were the children.

A small tot sat atop the rubble that had been his home, sobbing bitterly. I approached him, talked to him gently, stroked his tangled curls. The sobbing went on. Not a word would he speak.

The road climbed to a curve in the hillside. Alongside of us other houses lay in heaps of broken masonry. The front wall of one rose stark against the sky. I glimpsed the blue of the sky framed in the skeleton windows. Among the ruins green grass stretched tender blades.

A man passed, walking hurriedly, under his arm a load of wood, broken ammunition boxes. Without a glance at us he went on his way. A woman in black came next, a tub filled with water on her head.

"Whose boy is it?" she asked.

"I do not know," I answered.

"One more, alone in the world," and that was all.

Somehow I knew that her words, crude though they sounded, held no real coldness, no lack of compassion.

I took the child in my arms. He told me his name, that his parents lay buried under the rubble.

In the Salesian Institute one of the patients was an orphan of ten who had also lost a dear one in a bombardment. He was rather small for his age. A keen intelligence showed in his blue eyes. Every day he walked to the little street in Genzano where his house had stood. On one of his trips he watched the German workers as they dug in the ruins of a shattered building hoping to salvage a deposit of cigarettes they had been told was there.

Suddenly the boy started to tremble, his face white and tense. Under the strokes of the hammers a large piece of masonry broke and fell apart disclosing a mass of blond curls. Silence for an instant, then the broken sobs of the boy. It was his sister.

A continuous lesson was taught to us during that agonized time of how many barriers a real feeling for the brotherhood of man can surmount. How closely it can knit men of the most diverse opinions, political or otherwise, how social differences can be leveled when danger strikes.

Innumerable souls fought for the betterment of their neighbors. Citizens of high and low degree united, childless women, made so by the war, gathered homeless little ones wandering hopeless and lost in the street and on the road and mothered them.

Paradoxically perhaps, a sense of deep pity, a Christlike charity burst forth from the hatred of man for man, from a war, unleashed by the ferocity of opposing factions, by men fighting with the most modern of lethal methods and with the cruelty of savages. The basic goodness in the hearts of men rose to the surface and would not be stilled. The words of the apostle were given heed: "Ye must not love with words alone, but with deeds, with the diffusion of truth."

In the meantime, other devastated regions appealed for aid.

The territories of Frosinone, Cassino, and Terracino were without doubt the worst hit. Since we had done all that could be done for the present in the Castelli region, we betook ourselves to the new areas.

I did not recognize them. The scourge had left only ruin, misery, starvation. Near Cassino, I found the houses, fields and forests leveled to the ground. Not only that. Huge bomb craters riddled it.

The inhabitants of towns and small villages, I was told, had scattered and lived in the new way . . . underground. The story of the Castelli repeated itself a dozen, a score of times, with the added danger of a closer contact with enemy fire. The lost children here rose to staggering numbers.

Near Cassino, the main highway runs for many miles beyond Aquino. The vegetation of the hillsides had been luxuriant, rich with vineyards and olive groves in impressive contrast to the craggy rocks uplifted over them.

On that long road, the end of it lost in groves of trees barely discernible to the naked eye, the murky, cloudy morning restless with the thunder of cannon, the hiss of shells traveling over our heads, told us that Cassino was under heavy bombardment. We dared not be on that road.

Far in the distance two tiny black dots moved toward us. They approached slowly and moment by moment took shape and size.

Nearer and nearer till we made out a small boy and a still smaller girl, hand in hand, blond, delicate of feature, smiling at each other, but their eyes empty and devoid of any expression.

In tatters, eyelids swollen with weeping, caked with dust and dirt from head to foot. We stared at them, our hearts sick with pity. They looked at us unseeing and kept on going.

I stopped them and spoke. Not a word, not a sound, only those vacant smiles. I lifted them into my car. Silence still, but they did not resist me.

In Rome they were given shelter. I went to see them and I found them in the same condition. No one has to this day been able to learn who they are, whence they came, or what was the tragedy in their baby lives.

Hundreds of these children died from hunger and exposure. I recall one case which in stark horror exceeds anything I had seen or heard of. It was told to me by an Allied officer.

The scene was one of the peasant homes built on the slope of a hill near Terracina. The animals had been taken or killed, the farm implements lay scattered on the ravaged field. Bombs had reduced the house to a shambles. Part of it still stood. The door hung on one hinge.

Sitting on the floor of what had been a bedroom, pieces of plaster and broken furniture all around her, sat a child of eight. On the mattress of the only bed lay three tiny skeletons, bare skin their only covering . . . her little brothers. Over the bed several family photographs. One of them showed a man in the uniform of a corporal of the infantry . . . the father who had fought no doubt on some foreign soil, dreams of them spurring him on. The inscription at the bottom of the photograph read: "To my beloved children, from your loving father." The signature was signed in full.

"Where is your mother?" the officer had asked the little girl.

She had not known.

In the silence and the desolation, the wail of a child, the characteristic, tearless sobbing of childhood persisted.

The work in the two areas curtailed my duties at the Hospital of Via Monserrato, although I tried to be there at least two days a week. For a time this hospital continued to care for wounded soldiers, then it handled civic cases exclusively, but in spite of this it was always filled. The wards were jammed with air-raid victims, some of their wounds were so horrible they do not bear description. I recall mere bundles of breathing flesh, without hearing, sight, speech, or the will to live.

To re-enter the doors of Via Monserrato where the children had been taken was like returning home. The tragedy was not so stark here. Love wandered through its halls, sat at the bedside of a child. The cold hatred of the ravaged countryside, the mud, the anguish in the eyes of the people, faded from my heart.

The sight of the child victims was hard to bear, however. They lay in small wards, four beds to a ward. They neither cried nor complained, the silence was almost unreal. Several, badly burned by the incendiary bombs, had been bandaged from head to toe and looked like human snowballs. I thought of the older invalids who sometimes cried out against fate. Unlike them, these little ones were satisfied to lie quiet in the hospital room, on the white softness of the mattress, under the touch of a tender hand.

In my thoughts I associated them with the hundreds I had met in my wanderings. They revealed a whole new world to me . . . a world filled with young victims. They had been hurt in their hearts, in their souls, in their belief in a kind world. Would it be possible to prevent this on some future day? Would it be necessary to wage another war that children might be guaranteed eyesight, that young mothers might glory in the unbridled joy of their little ones, as they watched them romping heedlessly through a field in bloom? Would we have to fight and struggle on that hate might not kill, that love might purify, that the natural anxieties of daily existence might not include those of fear and terror?

This could be brought about only in a seeking after God and finding in His Fatherhood the brotherhood of man. This and this alone could bring about the triumph of humility, of meekness, of charity and peace. False ambitions, dreams of expansion and the pride that brings about conflicts could then be banished forever.

In the meantime, war still exists in the world today and we who suffer as we ponder upon its effects, can still pray and work that this may come to be. Our power lies in that.

II

FLASHBACK

II

FLASHBACK

"The fathers and mothers of the war, killed and
wounded and maimed have handed on a sacred
trust to protect the orphans and the homeless. . . ."
                                                    V.M.C.

I HAD HAD MY FIRST AWAKENING TO THE GREAT WAR
in 1940. I often went to the railroad station in Rome
to bid farewell to the students who were leaving to join
their families in the countries of their origin before Italy's
entry into the great conflict.

Uniforms, uniforms everywhere and people with vacant
looks in their eyes. A mother's tears and the sad songs
of the Alpine troops, their knapsacks stuffed with socks
and scarves knit by loving hands, with biscuits, with
sweets. Self-control here, despair a few steps away. A guard
who with infinite patience answers the questions three
blond gray-eyed giants from Venetia put to him. A tall
man, a straight martial figure embracing his young son,
white, tearless. "Do your duty, son," I heard him say. And
finally a captain calling his men to order.

The train is ready, the doors click closed, a more notice-
able blowing of noses, a murmur of voices rising gradually and becoming almost a roar in the final farewell. Two
sharp blasts of a trumpet and the train rushes off, taking

with it the dreams of a father, the hopes of a mother, the youth of men who may return . . . some of them . . . with wrinkles on their faces, wrinkles in their hearts.

Across the passageway on another track, a second train slowly fills up with young college boys, they, also, caught in the mighty avalanche that is sweeping them from Rome toward an unknown destination.

The two iron monsters gave me a sad forecast of the coming struggle, of the abandonment of all that is dear and precious to the human heart, of fond studies delayed, of family ties broken. Thoughts welled up in my heart, which later matured in prayer and led me toward my future work.

From that day I knew in the innermost recesses of my heart that war had struck.

War. It was among us, in our cities, in the sparsely scattered, humble cottages of the mountains and hillsides, in the wide stretches of the sea, in the clear blue of the skies, in dark clouds, on high, white, piercing peaks. It was in the words we exchanged with one another, in our actions. We found it in the Roman square where a huge black mass of silent, closely packed humanity heard the declaration of war on June 10, 1940.

The rumors that had assailed the city in the painful waiting and steeled souls to meet the inevitable had quieted down, but for a short time only, as if everyone was too stunned with grief even to think. Then life and death reigned again, but in their worst aspects.

I continued to work in the Sacred Congregation of

Seminaries and Universities where I had originally been appointed. My work tended to increase rather than diminish. I felt, like everyone else, the preoccupations, the anxieties, the difficulties the war was fostering.

However, in those long months, Rome still seemed an oasis of peace. Returning home at night, walking along the Lungotevere Boulevard, under the great, shadowy, century-old trees, the setting sun slowly moving toward the majestic cupola of St. Peter's as it sank to its rest, listening to the intermittent ringing of hundreds of church bells, I was at peace although a vague feeling of oppression sought to dim the incomparable vision of beauty I beheld.

Amid the chaos of war news that soon flooded the capital, I began to feel useless. Millions of men were dying, suffering, and I, we who lived "ad latere," on the side lines as it were, had no opportunity of alleviating their tortures, of coming to their aid, unless we did it with our prayers. But, was that enough?

Thus, when in January of 1941, the Sovereign Military Order of Malta, following its ancient tradition in the founding of hospitals, opened its first home in Rome and I was asked to become part of it as voluntary chaplain, I welcomed the opportunity offered me of serving my fellow man.

A few months later, the Order of Malta had to its credit a great number of other hospitals in Italy and throughout the world. Its trains, its first-aid stations were ready and waiting. Yet it is with a sense of humble pride that I say that our hospital, situated in the heart of medieval and baroque Rome, in the venerable English College of Via Monserrato, was second to none in the splendid work it carried on.

The four years within its walls were perhaps the happiest of my life. This may sound paradoxical, but it is true, for they were years in which, though witnessing the most frightful scenes, the most heart-rending tortures, I also beheld the spirit of man, luminous with faith and fortified by grace, rising triumphant over the weaknesses of the flesh. They were years I lived in direct contact with torn, bleeding humanity, when I experienced the full joy of being able to console, to be the instrument, humble and unworthy thought it was, of an ever-loving, ever-merciful Father.

The Epiphany of 1941 was a real feast day for me, for on that day I was granted the privilege of assisting at the bedsides of men, sick, wounded, alone, and helpless, comforting them, lifting their hopes. From that day, a foggy gray day, I could not help noticing how in those long, white, silent wards, there was none of that typical coldness so often found in similar places.

In general, invalids lose part of their identity in a hospital ward and are identified only by a clinical card, a diagram, a number over their beds. Here in Monserrato there was an aura of family life, as it were, that broke the monotony of our duties and made us all brothers — doctors, nurses, sisters, patients, helpers — linking us into a better understanding of what human brotherhood should be when a common grief or a simple joy is shared. Everyone was animated by the same spirit of charity, all without exception showed how such a spirit never fails to work miracles.

The doctors, all close friends of mine, were as fathers and brothers to the men to whom they gave, not only medicine for their broken bodies, but encouragement for their shattered souls. The nurses of the Order of Malta, all volunteers and most of them belonging to some of the oldest families of Italy, had adapted themselves to their arduous task with an ease that showed the serene and joyous spirit within. They had no thought of spending their days in the social halls of the capital between a cocktail party and a game of bridge. They moved silently from cot to cot, real angels of mercy and love.

The patients themselves, even from the first days of their stay, felt this atmosphere of peace, of friendship and easy comradeship, and thrived under it. There were some, of course, who, embittered by their painful experiences, shied away from any attention. They were the ones who nurtured within their souls too deep a resentment against the fate that had deprived them of their youth, lost somewhere on the barren wastes of a battlefield, or on the craggy peaks of an Alpine pass. As a rule, however, the warmth that surrounded them did not fail, before too long, to conquer even these. At times they were almost gay.

The wounded came from Albania, where the battles had been fought amid the most cruel privations and sudden, unexplained orders. Caught in the piercing cold of the bleakest regions, utterly unprepared and poorly clad, they were brought in suffering from frostbite and gangrene.

On his return from an operating room, a crippled lad opened weary eyes and spoke in a halting, intense voice.

". . . we crawled on that night across a field . . . over barbed wire . . . under our clutching fingers, the face of a dead man fell apart. We went on . . . in our minds thoughts of home . . . wives, mothers, sons. . . . We barely saw the sergeant as he beckoned an order to us in the dark. The profile of an enemy sentinel stood out against the sky. . . . On and on still . . . a hand grenade and another and another burst into flame and lit up the whole place . . . explosions, shouts, mortars rumbled. I felt a prickling in my leg . . . it was like a hundred needles. . . . I flattened out behind a friendly rock . . . lucky for me it was there. . . . The fire kept on . . . lessened . . . then stopped. I dug my nails into the rocky soil. . . . If only I could have disappeared into the ground . . . away from it all . . . rotting bodies . . . no longer to smell . . . no longer to feel the helmet of a dead buddy digging into my belly. . . . Dawn broke . . . I started to crawl again . . . blood, dead eyes, bodies . . . more bodies . . . the stench of bodies falling apart . . . the piercing needles were gone . . . the med at last. . . . I passed out. . . . I woke up here. . . . I asked questions . . . well, Father, here I am, but no leg . . ."

We had one hundred and fifty major amputation cases and most of them had received first-aid only upon reaching the hospital. Albania stuck in their minds as their most bitter hour.

Even in Rome that year the winter was severe. We had little coal and the windows were kept closed. This intensi-

fied the suffocating foulness of the gangrenous flesh. From
early morning till far into the night the doctors operated
silently, efficiently, the only sounds the muffled roll of the
stretcher wheels, the labored breathing of the patients,
the steady puffing of the anaesthetic bag. I often asked
myself if this could possibly be a hospital in the center
of Rome. Was it not rather a field tent in some lost land?

The work went on incessantly. The doctors looked more
dead than alive.

"I can't take this much longer, Father. I feel like a
butcher. . . ."

It was a weariness of the spirit rather than of the body.
They were sick of it all, sick with the horror that never
ended, that kept on and on under their red-rimmed eyes,
their dripping fingers.

Those men became as my own sons to me. Each one of
them, even the most mature, was in need of affection, of
some one upon whom he could lean for strength, in whom
he could confide, and I felt I wanted to be near them if
they should ever ask for me. I had a deep admiration for
them, they were so patient and so brave in spite of their
terrible fate. One thing touched me particularly. Never
a word of hate for the enemy, only a sadness, a feeling of
utter helplessness face to face with the proof of the futility
of war.

Some revealed their characters between a joke and a
sigh. They opened hearts and minds to me and I was grateful, as grateful as were the hospital wards when the warmth
of the spring sunshine finally invaded them and the sun
broke through the gray.

In one room lay two men from Naples, one a young boy about twenty, tall, thin, his oval face still smooth. He was innately good, but a typical *scugnizzo* (Neopolitan street boy), who had not lost the sly, mordant wit of his kind. Coupled with his evident candor, this made him appear at times slightly unbalanced. He was suffering from a strange ailment which the doctors had been unable to diagnose. One foot was slowly decaying. His name was Ciro. The other was much older, stockier. A thick black mustache and beard almost covered the lower part of his face. He was a non-commissioned officer and fairly well educated. We listened to him as he lectured Ciro with a ceremonious air that irritated his younger companion.

"That's no way to act . . . why don't you do this? Why don't you say that? You keep this up, son, and you'll end up bad. . . ."

"Ciro, what were you before the war?" I asked one day.

"A rascal."

"And your father?"

"A rascal."

He might or might not have been telling the truth. As he spoke, his eyes had the badgering look of the *scugnizzo*. I felt he was poking fun at me.

In the succeeding days I stopped often at their bedside. They both asked me to be present at the operating table.

"You'll bring us luck, Father," urged Ciro.

Several days later another patient made the same request and then another and another. Soon it became a habit. I spent four or five hours a day in the operating room. Sometimes, at the end of a particularly long session, my head reeled from the ether fumes as I emerged from the room.

I could not stay away. These boys wanted me. Far from their homes and their dear ones, they needed the words of a priest, a joke, a tear, a laugh, a prayer, someone with whom they could share their buried thoughts, a brother to whom they could turn, one who had no professional orders to obey, no scalpel in hand, no saws, no shears. Above all, one who could take the words of Christ and through them give suffering and pain their spiritual value.

They clung to my hand as they fell asleep under the anaesthetic.

"Father . . ." as they awoke.

"Steady, son, life is still good. . . ."

"But, Father, my right arm is gone. How will I be able to work?"

The table again, the knife, more blood, more bandages. Will this ever stop? Will this slaughter go on forever?

The hearth, the center of the world for these boys was always in their minds. They told me of their parents, their wives, their children, their simple joys at the village fair. They were naïve lads, with a naïve outlook upon life that was often disconcerting. Deep in their hearts and in their souls I found so much real goodness.

I recall one young fellow who proudly handed me a new book, straight out of a nearby store where one of the hospital aides had bought it for him.

"Father, will you find a good letter for me in there? I have to write to my *innamorata*.

I looked at the book. *One Hundred Letters of Love,* I read.

The doctors enjoyed discussing their operations with me and the problems that confronted them. They seemed glad to find a priest with a technical interest in the daily routine. I was not for them just another colleague, whose cases were fixed within fixed and rigid lines. In my presence the outlines of small things faded into the whole and the operating table was forgotten. They often grumbled when patients refused to be operated on unless I was present, but at night as we paced up and down the long corridors we chatted and found time and energy for a laugh and a joke.

Along toward midnight I usually wandered around alone. Before entering a room, I would stand at the door listening. I often heard a patient battling aloud with future problems.

"Father, it's hard to sleep," they said to me.

We chatted. Words were hard to say. Their hearts were so filled with bitter thoughts, but their spirits won in the end. It was hard to smile, but they did.

One task stood out as one of the most difficult I had to face. Many refused to write and tell their fathers or mothers of their real condition. It was often my job to meet them and tell them of the loss of arms or legs when they came to visit their sons.

Such were perhaps the saddest moments of the long sad days.

A wife and her children came to see the husband and father. He was the cheerful one.

"What are *you* complaining about? Won't I be home

soon? Won't everything be all right then? Minus a leg? With a good wooden one, I'll be as good as new. . . . I'll do twice as much as before. . . . I'm alive, eh? What more do you want?"

And strong women came who on hearing bad news gave their sons the smiles they had been waiting to see.

"Nothing matters now . . . you are with us again . . . that's enough . . . they can't take you away now . . . we'll get along. . . ."

The home. They focused their eyes upon it, near or far. All they asked for was to return there. They showed me photographs of their small cottages, their children . . . they never stopped talking about them.

"He has black hair, Father, and the littlest, littlest nose," Battista said to me each time I caught him studying the picture of his small son. "How he must have grown!"

The reunion was not to take place. One morning I received a telegram. The little fellow had died, from hunger probably. No one was willing to break the news to Battista. I had to go to him.

The room was bright with sunshine, the spring sunshine that in March pours so warmly over Rome. Battista was reading a newspaper. I sat down beside him and laid my hand on his shoulder. That was all. He knew. A sixth sense must have prompted the questions he put to me.

"Bad news, Father? Something happen to him? What is it?"

"Yes . . ."

He knew somehow. And we said nothing more. He grasped my hand, held on to it as sobs rocked his big frame.

"Why? Why?"

The sun shone on. One beam was reflected from the water in the bottle on the table near his cot. The Christ from the cross hanging above him seemed to cast a look of infinite pity upon the bowed head. . . .

Particularly touching to me was the dark-skinned boy from Somaliland. We called him Mohammed.

He was gravely ill, the only African boy among all the other patients. His dark face cutting the white pillow, his eyes wide open, he followed every move of those about him. Nothing we could do in the way of care was of any use and he grew steadily worse. The end was not far off. He knew only a few words of Italian, insufficient for any request, for any conversation, and he went on suffering, silent and lonely.

"Wounded as he is, he must be going through the tortures of the damned, but he has a strong will and he does not complain," the doctors said of him.

Thinking him a Catholic, a good nurse gave him a rosary, but on seeing the cross he turned away in aversion. He was a Mohammedan.

Whenever I visited him, I had a feeling of embarrassment. I did not know what to say to him. I could not speak a word of his language, he little of mine. I tried to convey to him that I understood what he was undergoing.

One night the doctor called me to tell me the end was not far off. I hurried to him.

As I watched the man's agony, I wished for some means by which I could give him a measure of comfort. His strength was ebbing fast. His eyes were closed and I thought him asleep. His breathing became irregular.

Suddenly, eyes still closed, he drew one hand from under the sheet and made a blind gesture, as if seeking something. I gave him my hand. He clasped it tightly to his breast and covered it with his other hand. I could feel his heart beating, still strong, but gradually it slowed. He had lost consciousness. A few moments later he died.

As I have said before, sadness was not the all-invading force in the hospital. Life varied, taking color from the different personalities who dwelled there. Some of the boys had almost unconsciously taken upon themselves the task of lifting the morale of their companions. They laughed uproariously as they played tricks on one another. This happened frequently, especially in the officers' quarters. The traditional jokers were there as they are in every college dormitory or soldiers' barracks.

One evening an officer who was fully recovered was given permission to leave the hospital for a few hours prior to his being discharged. In his absence his colleagues in the ward took a white marble bust of Pope Leo XIII from its niche in the corridor and placed in the officer's bed, the head snug on the pillow, the bedclothes bundled under the sheet.

The officer returned about ten o'clock. The ward was quiet and in almost complete darkness. Only the blue night light glowed. Every man in the room was wide-awake and waiting.

On tiptoes not to disturb his friends, the officer enters,

walks over to his cot, and sits down to slip off his boots. His hand goes to the pillow to pull down the sheet. Stifling a cry, he stares down for a moment then dashes down the aisle and out into the corridor.

A few moments later the barefoot boy returns with some one in tow. It is one of the Sisters, a small fussy bundle of nerves who simply cannot understand how such a thing could have happened in so well-organized a place.

She bends over the pillow.

"Dear God, help! He is dead!"

Her high-strung voice rings out in the silent ward. A roar of laughter and a flood of light as one of the men surreptitiously turns the switch. Even the little nun who hurries away red with confusion is not wholly displeased at the success of the prank.

At times it was apparent that the gaiety was feigned. You felt that laughter hid tears and you thought of the wrong note of a violin spoiling an otherwise perfect passage. However, the deep joy in spiritual things, revived and fostered in the friendly atmosphere, grew stronger day by day and men who had suffered turned to their God in the battle for life.

A number of our patients tore away completely from the patterns of their former lives. Confined within those walls, immersed in a sea of pain, they were forced to seek out the true meaning of life. They soon came to realize that beyond a purely material existence there is a higher life, a more sublime one as revealed by faith. Many, the greater number, bowed submissively to the fact that suffering accepted in the name of God and for love of Him and of our fellow man is one of the greatest builders of character in man.

An admirable example of this I found in Ottone, a young soldier. His clinical card showed not only the progress of his malady, but also gave detailed information of his early years. It was not difficult to see that he had led a highly disorganized existence.

His glance was sullen, the toughness of his character revealed by the sharp bitter replies he gave anyone who questioned him. Never a word of gratitude for the nurse who took care of him. For the men assisting him he reserved his most cynical remarks, for the doctor doing his utmost to relieve his pain nothing but complaints, for the chaplain a frozen indifference. No one liked him, as he did not spare even his own buddies.

He had been brought to the hospital on a questioned prognosis. In a few days the signs of an unconquerable disease manifested themselves and the dissolution of his body began, slow and inexorable. The rotting flesh fell piece by piece, his arms, his legs showed as mere bones.

Ottone sat on the edge of his bed, day and night, night and day, thinking. Two basins under his feet filled slowly with blood, bits of skin and muscle. Unable to lie down, he tried to rest propped up with pillows.

The tortures he had to undergo never ended and I visited him often. Nurses and doctors gave him their most assiduous care, but the bitterness, the harshness in his character persisted, intensified by the thought of what life might have been for him. Among so many other great sufferers, his attitude stood out as unique.

To make matters worse for him, a further examination

one day revealed the fact that he had also contracted tuberculosis. For the safety of the other patients, he had to be removed to a sanatorium on the outskirts of the capital. It was sad to think that the new surroundings would probably add to his sense of loss, of abandonment.

I made up my mind to visit him in his new quarters. Although the sanatorium was at a considerable distance from our hospital, I was able to make several trips there. Later I visited him every day.

How it happened I could not at first explain to myself, but I began to notice signs of a change in the boy. Not in his physical condition — that was beyond human endeavor — but in his outlook upon life.

In the succeeding months he gradually lost most of his cruelty. His replies were more controlled, he expressed less hatred for everything and everyone. I noticed that as his life slowly ebbed, he was acquiring a greater serenity, a vivid touch of grace. The natural goodness in him was rising to the surface.

Another operation was attempted and I watched its progress. He bore it calmly and with courage. To relieve his suffering, both his legs were amputated.

I sat at his bedside after the ordeal. I saw the relaxed lines of his face, his hands, thin, waxy, almost diaphanous. As I had entered his room, I had felt the new atmosphere of the place.

Ottone was now well liked. Not only that. The influence of his indomitable spirit in the face of his sufferings was beginning to be felt throughout the ward. He had made his peace with his God. Prayer and the sacraments had become necessary for him and he was offering his sufferings in expiation for the salvation of the world. What had wrought the miracle was so simple and yet so limitless.

I saw the head nurse after leaving him one day. It had become a habit with me to stop at her office for the cup of coffee she graciously offered me whenever I came to the hospital. She was a fine, strong character, capable and good. On that particular day I noticed that something was wrong. I had not long to wait for an explanation.

"Father, I can't stand it," she suddenly burst out.

"What's wrong?"

"That poor Ottone in that room . . . the torture he's been undergoing . . . it isn't fair. Why does a God who is supposed to be merciful allow it? My faith is beginning to waver, Father. . . ."

A wave of happiness surged up in me. At last someone had given definite expression to the great *"Why?"* of the moment. To the why asked by the wounded of Albania, to the why whispered by Adrian and his mother, to the why sobbed out by Battista who had guessed the news of his little son's death.

Ottone's relaxed face came back to me, the smile he had turned to me as I left his room.

"Sister," I answered, and I smiled as I spoke, "if I had any doubts myself, this case alone out of many others would be sufficient to dissipate them, to confirm my faith. You and I have seen this boy as he was when he first entered these doors, you have read his story on the clinical record, you have experienced the bitterness, the hate with which his whole being was charged. And now? Tell me, what is it that has brought about this change in him, if not the bending of his head to God? He has simply accepted the means God saw fit to give him for his own redemption. . . ."

A day came when I visited Ottone for the last time. I was leaving on the following day for Portugal and Ireland.

"Ottone," I said to him, "I must bid you good-bye now, but I shall return soon. What do you want me to bring you from my country?"

He took my hand in his thin white one and smiled, gazing at me fixedly for a long time. Although he was much younger than I, I saw in his look both a deep wisdom and a quality akin to the blessing of a father. In that small hospital room there was joy as well as pain.

"When you return, Father, I shall not be here," he said very low.

A moment of suspense, an instant that stretched into eternity and he added, even lower:

"When I am in paradise, I shall remember the Irish priest who came to see me. . . ."

I clasped his hand, rose and closed the door softly as I walked out. I never saw him again.

On the plane which was taking me to Rome, I opened a small book an officer had handed to me as I left. I had seen many of my patients reading it lately.

"There is no conquest without suffering . . . no rising without suffering . . . no reward without suffering. I ponder on the suffering in the world of to-day . . . it has a hundred faces, a hundred expressions, but springing forth from all this sorrow, all this pain, a great flame is rising toward the Almighty, a fire of burning hope that Love may come again. Love in sorrow, Love for sorrow." *

After four years of my uninterrupted stay in Italy, I was happy to be going home to Ireland.

Accustomed as I had been for so long a time to the harsh exigencies of war and to the sacrifices that war imposes upon those who live away from the battlefront, this trip offered a new vista of life to me.

The Avenida de Liberdate in Lisbon stretched before me in all its cosmopolitan splendor, breathing an unconscious, free joyousness. I met no one on the wide boulevards, if not men, women, and children on whose faces happiness and a belief in life was still clearly written. There were no seas of uniforms, no mourning wives and mothers as I had met everywhere in Italy, where the very air was pregnant with tortured thoughts. Life was natural and easy. People came and went, laughing, chatting, their zest for gaiety springing spontaneously from a sense of security.

The whole spectacle gave me a feeling of peace and well-being and yet it often brought back to my mind the vision of horror in so many other places, the anguish, the ruin. Lisbon was an island in a sea of blood and tears.

I found myself in this part of the world at a time when Italy was slowly being crushed under the wheels of war. Day by day in that unfortunate land the unmistakable signs of the crumbling Axis grew and increased.

Once again I saw Dublin, my mother, my relatives, my friends, but even this did not succeed in wiping out of my

* Nino Salmaneschi

mind the thought of Rome. My state of mind became gloomier the day I was told of the bombardment of the Basilica of San Lorenzo. Event piled upon event in the Italian peninsula and among them the fall of the Fascist regime on July 25, 1943.

I had made plans not to return to Rome until the end of September. The doctors there had told me I needed a prolonged rest. The headlong sweep of events in Italy, however, and particularly the landing of American troops in Sicily made me change my mind and return immediately.

My mother faced the news of my decision with calm serenity, although my absence, she realized, was to be a lengthy one.

On August 11, the day I landed in Italy, I became aware of the tension in the faces of the people I met, of a sort of expectancy in the atmosphere. Danger was not a mere chimera of a fanciful imagination. It was real. Some looked forward to a solution, others feared it. In the continuous seesawing of ideas, rumors were whispered, suppositions aired and then came the fateful date of September 8, when Italy signed the Allied armistice.

There was unbridled joy for a moment, but this joy was quickly shattered by the bad news seeping into the capital and by the reality of horror which in the space of a few hours showed its tragic countenance.

The announcement of the armistice signified for most of the people of Rome a return to normality, the end of terror, of privations, of air raids. It meant peace and more abundant food for their children. All these hopes soon vanished.

On the night of September 8 and during the early hours of September 9, we heard the first distant rumblings of cannon shots. Optimistic souls attributed the sounds to the order given for the demolition of coastal defenses.

"They are tearing down the forts," was heard all around.

No one thought of the German attacks against the Italian positions which the Italian Army had set up for the defense of the capital. One rumor said that the British had landed at Ostia and would be in the capital within a few hours. Few seemed to realize the whole truth. The armistice had caught everyone, leaders, soldiers and citizens utterly unprepared. Few visualized that Rome would have, and soon, a number of battles to wage. The Germans, furious at the turn of events, attacked the city from within and without; traitors did their nefarious work wherever and whenever they found fertile soil; the Allies made plans to take the city sooner or later.

"Peace! Peace!"

The word was on everybody's lips and war was drawing inexorably closer, ready to sweep everything into its deadly fury. Within a few hours Rome was to undergo inconceivable sufferings in the ferocity of a conflict we were to know only too well as the maimed and the wounded poured into the hospital in a never-ending stream.

That night most of the medical staff had gone home to snatch a few hour's rest. The preceding night they had waited vainly till dawn for the war casualties that might have come, but had not arrived.

Those of us who were left sat around waiting. It was late and I was about to retire to my room. An unusual tremor shook the building. Alarmed and tense, we rushed to the doors.

An armored tank had slid to a stop with screaming brakes. A young officer leaped out and gestured dazedly toward the seat of the car. We found his companion bleeding and unconscious.

He was the first. Others followed in quick succession. Tanks, trucks, ambulances stopped long enough to disgorge their mangled cargoes, and off they dashed, only to return with more . . . more . . .

And more fatigue, more horror. It was the old story repeating itself, operations and death, the old evidence of a useless hatred.

The wounded gave us news that kept getting worse and worse. The Germans had reached the Tre Fontane . . . only three miles from the center of the city. . . . They are at the Gate of San Paolo . . . they are coming closer. Some even said that they were in one of the squares of the capital.

About midnight I went out with a friend. We were anxious to find out how matters really stood.

During the day, Rome had been a ghost city. It had all the appearance of a city struck by an epidemic. Stores were barred, panic was in the sudden rush of an ambulance and was in the complete absence of the traditional carts. Panic also in the faces of the few pedestrians scuttling here and there in search of a hiding place from they knew not what.

In normal times, Rome differs from the rest of the capitals of the world. At nine o'clock at night her streets are usually deserted. She seems to be disdainful of so-called night life. Toward midnight she comes alive for a moment. Theaters and concert halls open their doors and fill the streets. That night we saw no one.

As we approached the Piazza Venezia we did catch sight of a man, but at the sound of our motorcycle, he fled down one of the streets that flank the palace and disappeared.

In the vast square I saw a number of armored cars, but no drivers sat at the throttles. Silence, nothing but silence, broken now and then by the roar of a cannon or cut by the sharp ack-ack of a machine gun. I could not help comparing the place, so still in the white moonlight, with the picture of the teeming thousands that a short time before I had seen gathered under a certain window. . . .

The machine guns were coming nearer. The Piazza Venezia is not very far from the San Paolo Gate where the battle was in its final stages. The regular soldiers who formed part of the Italian defenders were about to abandon the gate after stiff resistance. In the confusion brought about by order and counterorder, some thought that Rome would surrender. Others spoke of making the capital an open city.

The San Paolo Gate cuts an immense square in two. Outside the walls at one side of the gate stands the pyramid of Caius Cassius. On the other side a road runs toward Ostia. Here the soldiers had fought, but they had not been alone. Men, women, and children even had joined in the fray. Armed with guns, knives, rifles taken from the dead and wounded, hand grenades and with bare hands, they gave a good account of themselves.

In the Via Ostiense at the end of the battle I had proof

of the heroism of mere children. Two boys lay dead, their
hands still clutching the incendiary bombs they had been
ready to hurl at the powerful German tanks. Not far from
them I spied two others, their pitiful small bodies riddled
with bullets. All the clothing worn by one of them con-
sisted of an old coat in shreds, bloody, and a pair of dirty
trousers. He was covered with wounds and bruises. He
lay on his side, face blown to bits, but brown curls dragging in the mud of the curb, in his fingers a piece of torn
leather belt. A few steps farther, on the same curbstone,
sat four boys whispering, planning I knew not what. I
spoke to two others crouching behind a broken wall and
tried to persuade them to go home. They looked at me as
if they did not understand the words I said, but as I walked
away, I saw them disappear in the shadows.

I returned to the hospital. There among the new casualties I found a young carabinier, who had just been brought
into the ward. He was about eighteen, his boyish looks
contrasting strangely with the uniform he wore. So young
to be a defender of the law! Upon examining him, the
doctor found only a small wound. I heard that the internal
mischief done by one bullet had made the boy's case hopeless. At his bedside stood an older member of the same
corps, the lad's superior officer, unashamed tears streaming
down furrowed cheeks, his brown rugged hand holding
on tight to the younger smoother one.

His eyes questioned me. I made him understand the
seriousness of the case. It was pitiful to see the anguish on
the old carabinier's face, a man who had no doubt seen
many horrors and untold evil.

The atmosphere of the room weighed heavy with the tragedy of the hospital bed. The boy lay as if sleeping. I leaned over him and barely heard the words he was trying to say. They held so much and they have lingered in my mind in the years since that day.

"Life plays strange tricks, Father . . . only a short time ago, she was so happy . . . my mother I mean . . . she thought of me so safe in the city . . . I was so far from Russia or Africa. That's where my brothers are . . . and now . . ."

I gave him the last sacraments and they took him away to the operating table in a first attempt to save his life. The sight of that boy lying so still, his life in the balance, perhaps about to close as he stood on the threshhold of maturity, brought to my mind several lines from one of Matthew Arnold's poems:

> Like some rich hyacinth which by
> the scythe of an unskilled gardener
> has been cut, mowing the garden
> grass-plots near its bed, and lies,
> a fragrant tower of purple bloom . . .*

and my heart was heavy with the thought of all this splendid youth so wastefully destroyed.

In direct contact as they were with the painful incidents taking place around them, the maimed and the crippled soldiers in the hospital suffered intensely. The nagging thought that their sacrifices had been in vain added to their physical sufferings.

The man who dies from injuries incurred while saving

* *Sohrab and Rustum*

the life of a child from a burning building dies with a feeling of exaltation that he has given his life for that of another. The maimed soldier who has lost his legs or his arms on the field of battle can find courage in knowing that he has helped in the defense of his country.

But the maimed and the crippled of this war saw all their beliefs, their hopes, their trust die on that fateful September 8. The allies of yesterday were the enemies of today, and vice versa the enemies of yesterday had suddenly become allies. They heard of Italians helping the Germans, of other Italians fighting against them for the liberation of Italy. The ensuing confusion in their minds was great. Their spiritual anguish, bitter.

One day I stopped at a bedside. The boy who lay there looked at me and said nothing.

"Son, you are sad . . ."

He nodded.

"Life is full of questions, son, so full that they can be explained only through the message in the life of Our Lord. He has invited us to follow Him, but in that invitation there is no promise of material happiness in this life. He has taught us that the cross must be borne, sufferings, injustice. God permits this, for He respects the freedom He granted to men. We can choose a life of selfish interests or believe in what He taught and choose spiritual values. We can be thus steadfast in adversity and unafraid and prove our loyalty and the sincerity of our love for Him. One thing God never does permit and that is the absence of the possibility of doing what is right and gaining life eternal."

"But it has all been so useless, Father."

"If you are trying to say to me that the sacrifice you made has not given victory to your country, I agree with you. However, you have done your duty, as you were made to understand your duty. You have carried your cross. This should be your feeling of success. God will give endless value to your pain, and bring forth for you as well as for your dear land a day of redemption."

III

HEROIC HEIGHTS OF UNSELFISHNESS

III

HEROIC HEIGHTS OF UNSELFISHNESS

"... by the thousands who strong in their resistance
against misfortune, sorrow and temptation. ..."

IN THE MIDST OF ALL THE HORROR, I CONTINUED TO MEET
those who were sincerely dedicated to bringing about
a modicum of good out of so much evil. The greater marvel
was to be determined not by men steeped in evil by the
passions of the hour, but by the thousands who, strong in
their resistance against misfortune, sorrow, and temptation
stretched upward to such heroic heights of unselfishness.

The luminous and sublime example of the Holy Father
gave supreme comfort to these elect souls, to these apostles
of charity, whether they lived their quiet lives in a convent
or struggled on in their miserable hovels, caves, and grottoes of the war zones. He spurred them to ever greater
achievements.

Several years had passed since the day I had knelt before him at the close of the conclave which had elected
him Supreme Pontiff. Notwithstanding the passing of the
years, the depth of my feeling toward him was ever the
same. His personal austerity, the self-control that commands the respect of all, the tranquillity of soul that
transpires from his glance and has so strong an effect upon

anyone who comes in contact with him, the simplicity of his manner, his kindness, his understanding, the sweetness of his smile can never be forgotten.

Men of good will throughout the world looked toward Rome with veneration and hope. The Romans in particular held for him a sentiment of profound filial devotion.

The evident proof of the esteem in which the people of Rome held His Holiness was fully demonstrated in the manifestation of loyal devotion and affection the refugees and the native population gave him on March 12, 1944.

On that memorable date when the road to be traveled seemed hardest, while the proximity of the battling armies weighed heavily upon the city and the threat of an ever-increasing danger grew, while fear of a catastrophe tensed the hearts of men and women, his words poured balm upon their troubled souls. Bitterness was quenched by the comforting knowledge that protection was granted to them under the mantle of Peter.

A tremendous crowd filled the huge square, two-hundred to three-hundred thousand, men and women of all walks of life, of every political affiliation, hobbling old men, strong mature men, children, toddlers, babes in the arms of their mothers who held them close, tears on their gaunt cheeks.

Cold dampness from the air bit into the bone, the sky dark with clouds threatened rain, but this had not stopped them, nor had the probability of air bombardments or German incursions. They had heeded the call of the Father and come to the protector of the hopeless, the dispenser of God's charity, the Vicar of Christ on earth.

"We feel and recognize in the bitterness that fills our minds, how unequal and inadequate all human aid is, when compared to the excess of nameless misery that is engulfing us. There are misfortunes for which the hand of man, even the most generous one, is not sufficient."

The words of the Holy Father fell upon the assembled multitude from the balcony where a white figure etched itself clearly against the imposing façade. The gray of the sky, the gray of column and arch, the gray of the atmosphere enveloping Rome and the world was suffused with light by that pale slender figure, hand uplifted in benediction.

People applauded, trembled, wept, and prayed. After the benediction, in an atmosphere of silence that was almost overpowering, men, women, children seemed to have suddenly acquired a new lease on life. Heads were held higher, eyes looked less spent.

"It is not true that all is lost. He has said so."

The Holy Father had followed and encouraged the activities of the Medical Corps. After encouraging our efforts in a number of ways for the betterment of conditions among the homeless, he suggested that the time was opportune for a closer coordination among the workers.

Thus came about the Pontifical Commission for Aid for the Refugees. I was asked to become part of it, and was in this way able to continue my activities in the zones which had, as it were, become my own and where naturally I could carry on with greater efficiency.

On April 19, the day after the Commission was founded,

the German authorities sent out the order for the evacuation of several towns in the Castelli area.

These towns, as I have mentioned before, had been abandoned by the greater number of their inhabitants, but hundreds were still trying to eke out a meager existence in the ruins and the rubble.

It is a well-established fact that the Italians, those in the southern regions of the Peninsula especially, succeed only with the greatest reluctance in tearing themselves away from the hearth to which a long tradition binds them. This attachment is an almost patriarchal one, the Italian lacking to a certain degree the nomadic spirit present in younger races. The secular love of the soil is still alive in them, the soil of the ancestors who preceded them and who worked and suffered there to give life to succeeding generations. The ruins or even the cave close to the humble bit of ground that had been and they felt was still theirs, represented everything to them, family, homeland . . . ancient, present, and future hopes.

The problems that cropped up on the order of evacuation were serious and difficult to solve. The short time allowed, the threat of the concentration camp, the lack of means for the transportation of so many people, as well as the search for new quarters, increased the hardships and made the solution an almost impossible task.

However, much was accomplished. With the help of busses furnished by the holy see, close to eight thousand migrated to Rome, a number of these even finding a way of taking with them their household goods.

Tragi-comic incidents often took place on the trips. I

was riding one day on one of the busses that the Germans used for the transportation of workers assigned to the Anzio battle area. These men had the task of clearing away the ruins and also of constructing barbed-wire fences.

It happened that in spite of military orders to the contrary, the drivers, for a small fee, let civilians travel on the busses, when, empty, they made their return journey to the capital.

The seats had all been removed to provide more space. I sat on a huge box and listened to a goat, bleating pitifully in its hiding place behind a wooden chest.

There were six of us in all and the conductor had a hard time climbing over tables, bags and bundles while trying to collect his fares. Everything, including a number of cackling chickens and the bleating goat and what not belonged to a single refugee. He had succeeded in persuading the driver to allow him to board the bus with his lares and penates, although this was strictly against the rules.

The journey was proceeding smoothly for a time. Then, just as the road narrowed and became hazardous because of the presence of the constabulary and the German patrols, the motor developed trouble and we were forced to stop.

Fearing more trouble, the driver saw himself obliged to ask the evacuee to leave with his chickens, the bleating goat, the furniture, the bags, and the bundles.

"What am I to do now?" he wailed, but he had to obey.

Not a house around. Bare fields under a hot sky. Now and then cannon flashing in the distance.

It was a case of either waiting for hours or walking . . .

we decided on walking and started off toward Rome. We left our former companion on the bus sitting on a chest, his face thoughtful, but resigned. The chickens pecked contentedly in the field, the goat licked the milestone by the road.

Many of the refugees from the Castelli regions found a haven in Castel Gandolfo and the pontifical villa adjoining it in the surrounding park.

This summer home of the Holy Father was soon completely filled, as he had given orders that no one was to be refused. In consequence, the magnificent gardens lost much of their serene beauty and their peaceful orderliness. Lawns and flower beds lay trampled. Improvised tents dotted the landscape.

The stairs of the villa were lined with mattresses, every available space having been utilized. Even the throne room and the private rooms of the Pope were occupied. It seemed unbelievable that such a multitude could be accommodated. The place had become a veritable town in miniature, where men and women and children lived again in peaceful surroundings. And yet the cannon and the air raids did not spare it entirely.

On the day set for the final evacuation of the territory, I made a tour of inspection of towns and hamlets to assure myself that orders had been scrupulously obeyed and that no surprises lurked.

I arrived at one of them. I found a deserted village, a graveyard of homes succeeding one upon the other, cold, empty, most of them shells of their former selves. Shutters bolted and barred. A door or a blind, hanging from a single hinge, clattered to and fro, loud and harsh in the quiet. Thick grime and dust covered everything, as in the halls of an ancient palace abandoned for centuries. I had the impression that no order existed, no disorder, that among those lonely walls there breathed neither good nor evil, but that life stood still, mute in its solitary waiting, not useful, not useless, pitiful witness to our miserable, selfish littleness.

The only inhabitant of Ariccia who had remained there was the village priest. He had been born in the little town and to it he had given his whole life, all his efforts in helping and comforting his flock. I found him waiting for me on the steps of his small church. A few words of greeting and then we entered the sacred edifice and knelt to pray. After that short prayer, he arose and walked to the belfry tower. In the vast solitude, one by one the strokes of the angelus rolled out into the air, calling men to prayer, calling them back to God. It sounded in our ears alone and we raised our hearts to the Almighty, that an end might soon be put to the devastation. We prayed that the little church might once again be crowded with simple worshippers, devout souls, that streets might ring once more with the laughter and shouts of children chasing one another, that doors might be reopened, that the skeleton homes might come alive, that no passer-by might be aware of only one sound, the whining of a shutter, swinging on a single hinge.

At five o'clock sharp the death sentence was to be imposed on anyone found within the proscribed areas, so I hastened back, crossing the line at the established hour.

Later I obtained special permission from the German Command to visit these zones whenever I felt that it was necessary.

Ten days had been granted for the evacuation. Each transfer was preceded by the distribution of food sent by the Holy Father. Inadequate were these distributions, but so welcome and so helpful in those extremities when the small quantity of a gram of spaghetti or macaroni had inestimable value.

The women accepted the offering gratefully. Notwithstanding the tragic moment, they were happy and with them their little ones. They felt comforted by the fact that they could satisfy their most urgent needs, even if in so small a way.

In my contacts with the German authorities, the latter were finally persuaded of the impossibility of providing for the complete transfer of the refugees within the prescribed time. They acceded to my request for a longer period, but gave no official order for the concession. This was of great help as the evacuation was accomplished with more calm and with no added tragedies.

In the order given on April 19, no mention had been made of Lanuvio, a small town situated close to the battlefront. Its citizens were hopeful that the Germans, hard put as they were by more pressing and urgent matters, would forget about them. They stayed on, clinging to what was left of their homes, risking their lives under the threat of the continuous bombardments.

I cannot state with complete certainty whether the subsequent order on May 19 was good or bad for them. What frightened everyone was the way in which the peremptory order, "by three o'clock of this same day," was carried out. No means for transportation were provided. Furthermore, the town was blocked at all exits.

The population gathered at the appointed spot and on foot followed their guards to the concentration camp of Terre Gaia . . . Gay Tower. Paradoxical name!

The long column moved along in irregular formation. Women wept quietly, eyes staring straight ahead, not to see the abandoned home, not to think of the faraway husband. A child tugged at his mother's hand, gazing at her as if begging her not to cry. The aged pleaded for a moment's rest by the side of the road, longing not to take another step, not to suffer another pain, only to be allowed to close their eyes and perhaps wait for death as a liberation.

Thousands of episodes, thousands of misfortunes — how many had I witnessed! Forgotten people, lost people . . . everything gone . . . "and land, and home, and, save memory, all."

I met the sad procession and I approached the Salesian Father who walked disconsolately at the rear.

"Verboten!" sounded in my ear.

The German soldier, obedient robot, waved me on my way. I stood aside and stared at the winding, broken line disappearing down the long road, unable to lift a helping hand, to say a word, to caress a child, one of the many barefooted scrawny little beings that filed passed me.

In the meantime, in other towns, there was still the problem of the old and the very young. They had been left alone in their small worlds and now ran the risk of being sent to concentration camps.

While Father Feller, S.J., another member of the Pontifical Commission, tackled the problem in Rome with the Central German Command, I did what I could with local ones.

In my conversations with them, I had often discussed the situation of these people. I finally succeeded in reaching a solution. In a verbal agreement with the Germans, which naturally had no official character, it was stipulated that the aged, the children, and the sick would be allowed to stay on in the evacuated areas until we would be able to move them to a place of refuge, on condition, however, that they were to stay within the boundaries of certain institutions where they were all to be gathered together. Anyone who stayed outside these limits would be taken to a concentration camp.

The necessary work for the final transportation of these poor people took longer than we had expected and another difficulty arose. The food ran out and we had no means of obtaining more as the evacuation order forbade access to the zone.

Again I appealed to the German authorities.

A few hours later, the German soldiers themselves gave us part of their rations to feed those in our care. They kept their promise faithfully.

Father Charles Egger, a third member of the Refuge Commission and an indefatigable worker, had on many occasions accompanied the Vatican busses in dangerous trips to the North. He had made valuable contacts in various cities and towns of Central Italy, in the hope of being able to give definite help to many of the refugees. Many of the bishops, however, had been forced to refuse his plea as, just to mention Assisi, the localities at their disposal were by that time jammed to the doors with old and young.

The bishops of Gubbio and Città di Castello, towns in the region of Umbria, however, answered in the affirmative. These towns seemed particularly appropriate, situated as they were far from the principal roads. Besides, the Allied advance through Umbria was expected to be a rapid one. Sad to say, these hopes were not to be fulfilled.

In the beginning of May the trek began. This time the aged traveled in busses. Although they left all they possessed behind them, on finding themselves lovingly cared for by the Little Sisters of the Assumption and eating the food provided them, their worn faces brightened.

The superior, who with her Sisters had done so much in the town for the sick and the wounded, was difficult to persuade, when the moment came for her to decide whether or not to leave her cloister, her statue of St. Joseph, near the convent lake and the little church overlooking the panorama of valley and distant sea. She could not make herself believe that it was really necessary for her to break away from the place where she had spent most of her life after leaving her native France. She made up her mind at last and followed her old charges into exile. To tell the truth I did not have to insist too much.

In the subsequent weeks, the Home she had left behind was almost completely destroyed. Years later I saw it rebuilt and I met her again.

"Monsignor, you drove me into the hardest act of obedience in my whole life." She said this to me with a smile, referring, of course, to what had happened on that May morning.

On leaving, the children had a wonderful time. One incident amused us all very much. Among the Sisters, one was worried over the convent dog. It was a large shepherd, its long hair almost entirely white. Just as we were about to start, the little Sister insisted that the dog go along. There was a moment of perplexed waiting. I could not see how the animal, fine though he was, could travel along in the same conveyance as the old folks and the children. But the little Sister was stubborn and her stubborness lent a humorous note to the day. Heads hanging out of the bus windows, the children laughed gaily at the arguments. It was evident that they wanted her to win. That decided me. They wanted that dog. And so the dog became one of the passengers. He was a good old dog after all and the children's friend, as big dogs generally are, often growling at us older ones, but allowing their small tormentors the most unusual privileges.

One of these trips was rather turbulent.

At Castel Gandolfo there was a large house where many poor children had been gathered together. On May 29, it was decided to transfer them to Città di Castello in the Umbrian region.

I started out at dawn from Cisterna, where I had been

staying overnight in a cave, to reach Castel Gandolfo. About five o'clock I was caught under a sudden air attack the Americans were launching against the German positions. I sought shelter and luckily escaped any harm.

Not to run further risks, I took a roundabout way to my destination. It was an unfortunate choice. I had just reached the flat country around Lake Nemi, when a rain of machine-gun bullets pelted the road around my car. The marksman must have been having a good time with me, for the game became a little too accurate for my peace of mind. Again I came out of it safely.

At last I reached the Home, where I was to organize the departure and was about to stop, when I made a sudden decision to go first to the papal villa which was not too far away.

Hardly had I gone three hundred feet, when I came to a sudden stop, a sinking feeling clutching at my heart. A terrific explosion behind me made me fear the worst. My fears were realized in full. The Home I had just left with the waiting children had been hit by bombs. I could visualize only death and destruction. The thought of the little ones froze my blood with horror.

As soon as the bombers disappeared, I turned back and rushed to the scene. I found the youngsters cowering in the kitchen, a long, low building set apart from the Home. Some sat on the floor whimpering, others clung to the skirts of the two assistants. Dishes, cups, benches, and tables were white with plaster. One small boy stood near a table, drawing circles with the slow, unconscious movements of an automaton. Another toddled toward me from a corner.

"Father, I want to go home . . . my mother wants me . . ." she begged.

One by one they crowded around me, each with his own, particular request. Those who had run away to seek safety in the nearby forest drifted in from the open door, dazed with terror.

A child peeked in, pale, hair ruffled, not daring to enter, expecting no doubt that at any moment the kitchen would fall on top of him. His eyes wide with terror, he stared at his companions as if unbelieving that they could still be alive. He made no move to enter. I went to him, took him by the hand, led him to the others, asked him where he had been.

"Behind those trees . . . no one could see me . . ." and his mouth trembled pitifully.

In broken phrases he told of his adventure, of the droping bombs near where he hid. His heart beat fast with the excitement of the tale, but he did not cry. No strength for that.

Unable to do anything then, as a number of the children had not come back and could not be found, we decided to wait till four in the afternoon. Then I asked my small charges to line up in front of the ruined houses, so that I could keep an eye on them. They had eaten and calmed down considerably and were beginning to chatter among themselves, interested in what was going on.

In my hand I held a list of names. As each name was called, a voice answered, sharp and high or low and distracted. At each answer one of the assistants helped a youngster into the bus.

Again a roar and once more the planes flew overhead. The faces before me froze with renewed terror. A child burst into tears, an older girl started running toward the woods, most of my listeners forgot to answer. I continued reading, the women did their best trying to reassure them. But before they could be stopped, all of the children had streaked toward the trees and vanished. The only one left was the little tot who had been afraid to go into the kitchen and who had been close to me all day.

Another long wait. I sat down close to a low wall, the child in my arms. I tried to allay his fears. My words fell on deaf ears, deaf to them, but not to the crash and the uproar of the death from the sky. A thousand feet from us a tree was torn from the ground and blown clear away.

The women prayed out loud and at last there was quiet, but the quiet was filled with foreboding. What had happened to the children?

Suddenly my little friend burst into sobs, uncontrolled, racking, his fright, the tension of the day dissolving at last into tears. I was relieved. Better those tears and sobs than the wide-open eyes staring into space. At least I knew that his mind was not lost.

We relived the experience of a few hours earlier. One by one the children returned and without being told this time, took their places. I called the roll. Once, twice, a third time. Three did not answer.

The busses were filled, the motors running, the children, forgetting what had happened, were chattering and even laughing.

"Here we go!" they shouted.

Before leaving, I carved three names on a wooden cross, the names of the three little victims lying on the hillside. They would not again shout with joy, but neither would they tremble from the fear of death.

At a given signal the busses started. The children had suddenly become very quiet. Even the young understand that parting may be a time for reflection.

Our first stop was Vatican City. We arrived without further mishaps. A wooden barricade had been built around the great Square of St. Peter's and we went through the gate, the Swiss Guards on watch. It was a strange sight to see them carrying guns.

In the courtyard Cardinal Canali was waiting for his guests. The children were awed into silence, but as he came forward smiling they lost their self-consciousness.

They stood before him, dirty, ragged, pitiful, their faces still showing the strain of the day. The cardinal had given orders for a good meal to be prepared in the open. At the invitation to sit down at the table, eyes brightened and everyone looked expectant and happy. They sat down and ate hungrily. Now and then they raised their heads to gaze in wonder at the cardinal and at the members of the diplomatic corps, English, American, French, who had come down from their apartments in the adjoining palace and who gazed in pity on those starved small waifs.

By the end of the meal they talked and exchanged opinions. As we listened, we marveled at their mature reasoning. In a few months they had grown old, their acquaintance with cruelty and suffering and death had aged them far beyond their young years.

Months later I met some of these same children in a home for orphans. Many recognized me and seemed glad to see me. I reminded them of the tragic moments that had brought us together. By then, they had forgotten the horrors of war, or perhaps remembered them only as a vague faraway dream. They lived in comparative comfort at the time and the sad days had mercifully been wiped out.

The rest of the journey was successfully accomplished under the leadership of Father Egger. On the return trip, however, the busses, fortunately empty of children, were machine-gunned and one was demolished.

Shortly after the fourth of June, the day the Americans entered Rome, we heard that some of the children who had been sent to Gubbio were being held as hostages by the Germans and that, together with other inhabitants of the town, they had been taken to the Castle of St. Ubaldo, which overlooks the town.

That area was still in German hands, but I set out immediately, intending to wait until the Allies took the town and then to enter it and find out the truth. In a matter of hours my driver and I arrived at Umbertide. At the crossroads leading toward Gubbio, we came upon an English sentinel.

We stopped and asked him whether we could go farther along the road. He looked at us as if we were mad.

"The Germans are still in Gubbio," he remarked.

"Can we go a little farther along the road?"

"Go ahead if you like," he said shrugging his shoulders.

With this dubious permission, holding within it a warning and a piece of advice, we proceeded.

Beyond Rome the Allies pointed northwest and carried on operations through Umbria, on the road which, in its spurlike formation, bypasses the valley of Gubbio. The Germans had entrenched themselves on the citadel dominating the surrounding country.

We climbed the road and on reaching the top of the rise we drank our fill of the magnificent peaceful panorama flung out below us. The profusion of green, the wealth and luxuriance of foliage gave mute evidence to the justice of the praises the poets of Italy have showered upon "Umbria Santa," Holy Umbria as she is called.

In the background separated from us by a deep valley, Gubbio rose with its towers, its narrow streets, the russet of its walls cutting the translucent blue of the sky. This was the place where the humble Saint of Assisi had been able to tame even the wolves of the forest!

I told my driver I wished to go on by myself, not wanting him to run useless risks, but he refused to listen to me. Reluctantly, I nodded and we proceeded toward the bridge in the distance.

Silence, an ominous silence was all about us. At any instant we expected some kind of reaction from the Germans hiding in the hills above us. However, we reached the bridge and crossed it in safety. We covered the remaining distance in record time.

The Bishop of Gubbio, Monsignor Ubaldo, amazed to

see us, immediately assured me of the fate of the children. The reports had been erroneous. Not one had been taken as hostage. Gubbio and its inhabitants had not been so fortunate.

The retreating Germans had installed themselves in the northern part of the city and were using the belfry of the Basilica of St. Ubaldo as an observatory. In the church proper, they held close to 230 hostages, 70 children among them. These unfortunates had sought shelter there in order to escape the danger of air raids on the town. Their situation became critical, when the Germans, giving the proximity of the Allied forces as an excuse, prohibited anyone from leaving even for the purpose of procuring food in the city proper.

On July 3, the British initiated a terrific bombardment. Much damage resulted. Among the buildings struck was the cathedral and in this contingent, which protracted itself for twenty-four hours, the hostages were left completely isolated.

An attempt was made to send bread to them after an appeal to the German Command had brought the desired permission. As the volunteers reached the church, one of them was shot and killed by a German sentinel. This stopped all further efforts.

The situation of the hostages continued serious until July 24. On this day, the Germans suddenly withdrew from the town and the prisoners were freed. They were emaciated from the long fast, many not having touched food for two days. They pleaded for a piece of bread, and many fell from sheer exhaustion. Men and women wept for joy and lifted feeble voices in prayer, thanking God and St. Ubaldo, the protector of the town. They returned home hopeful for the future. Life went on.

The children who had come from Castel Gandolfo had been relatively lucky, in comparison to the seventy who had been for almost a month prisoners in the Basilica. Not so lucky had been the children sent to Città di Castello, which had its own share of suffering.

The opinion formulated by some that Umbria would be spared proved to be utterly false. On June 19, the German Command, in the merciless way we have often noted, ordered that Città di Castello be cleared of all inhabitants within twenty-four hours. The usual penalties were threatened for anyone caught disobeying the edict.

The bishop was at first denied permission to remain within the city limits. Later he was allowed to stay in his house, a virtual prisoner. Through his intersection, many of the religious communities were permitted to remain.

In one of these convents lived the children who had come from Castel Gandolfo.

One day the peace they had found was to be rudely shattered.

For thirty-two days aerial bombardments had succeeded one another without let-up. Grenades, howitzers, machine-gun bullets, tore apart, gutted, scorched the outskirts of the town. Forty-four bridges leveled, countless buildings pulverized, the railroad station reduced to an unrecognizable pile of stones and twisted iron.

The convent where the children had found shelter was in the heart of the city. Danger and lack of food made it advisable to remove them to another building on the out-skirts. This was done with all possible speed and caution.

The distance from the city gave assurance of a greater degree of safety from the raging battle. The little ones and the nuns were made as comfortable as possible in one of the wings.

Early one morning a half-dozen of the small tots were playing in the courtyard under the watchful eye of one of the nuns. There was the usual sound of distant cannon, but no one was paying any attention as even the noise of can-non can become a common, everyday sound. Besides had they not been told that they were far away and safe?

Without warning a new and more terrifying noise was heard, as of a giant wheel rolling clumsily along a pave-ment and meeting one obstacle after another. The trou-ble was that this pavement seemed to be in the sky. Louder, heavier, then an earsplitting crash . . . a blinding light, a terrifying roar . . . and in the courtyard . . . silence, followed quickly by heart-rending shrieks of pain and ter-ror.

The little girls scattered seeking a hole in which to hide, an avenue of escape.

In the middle of the courtyard lay a small body, an old dirty doll clasped close. A couple of yards away, another, and still farther on, the black-gowned body of the nun. No more games, no more dolls, no longer would these little girls play at "ladies," their laughter tinkling in the sun-shine. No longer would the other and older one nurse and bless and smile. Hate had seen to it that nothing of all this could ever happen again.

The transfer of the refugees from the Castelli areas was over. This allowed me to visit more often the concentration camps situated at Cesano and Torre Gaia. Both camps had an iniquitous reputation because of prevailing conditions and the complete isolation of the interned.

At Torre Gaia, immense barnlike sheds had been converted into huge dormitories. Thousands of refugees had been allocated there. They slept on the bare floors, as they had been obliged to leave behind them all of their household goods. No means or opportunity had been afforded them for taking along anything. Only a mere handful could boast of a little straw on which to lay their weary bones. No privacy existed. Family groups lived, ate, slept, where everyone else lived and ate and slept.

The children wandered about in a filthy condition, unwashed, uncombed, hair crawling with lice, many of them suffering from trachoma. In their wanderings, they did exactly as they pleased in the long, idle, endless hours of day or night.

–Early one morning I found myself on one of the roads which was most frequently strafed. If safety was to be given any consideration, the hours soon after dawn were the only ones that offered it to any degree. On that particular day I came to it just as a number of German busses arrived crowded with evacuees.

I helped an old man as he stepped out. Still fairly well groomed, he wore a dignified air, between that of a university professor and a family lawyer. I learned later that he was a doctor of medicine. All his near and dear had died. Seventy-five years of age, he had half a century of professional work to his credit. Entirely alone, he had considered his calling an apostolate.

In the little town in which he had spent all of his useful existence, simple, narrow perhaps, but not lacking in a certain ease, in gay, pleasant days, everyone including the oldest considered him the beneficent godfather, who year after year had given his counsel and advice, not restricted exclusively to his professional field.

The day before, he had seen his whole world crumble. His medicine cabinet, his tools, the little black leather bag he had not been allowed to take along in the hurried departure, some of his clothes, his best black ones, everything gone!

He told me all this in cultured, nostalgic speech.

"On my return I shall find nothing . . . my instruments, the ones my father gave me through the years while I was still at the university . . . those I shall miss most. . . ."

He gave the impression of a full life that had suddenly been snuffed out. I felt depressed as I sat listening to so old, so fine a human being and thought of the cruel blows fate had reserved for him in his late years . . . of how helpless, hopeless, and alone he was.

At the Cesano Camp it was an impossible feat to try to provide any amount of decent living conditions. There was little water and we felt utterly helpless in trying to prevent or care for the infectious diseases that soon developed in the close promiscuity.

The women, wretchedly clad, rose early as they had been accustomed to do in bygone days. There were no household tasks for them to attend to, however, nothing for them to work at, so they meandered here and there seeking the unseekable, eyes dull and lifeless, expressions vacant, foolish. They finally sat down near the spot where the daily rations would later be distributed and waited . . . sometimes for hours . . . far past the midday hour. And when the food did come, it was the same as the meal that had been served the day before and the day before that: soup, thin, watery, bread, poor, tasteless . . . and very little of either.

Sitting around in groups, munching, the youngsters talked of nothing but bread, real bread, macaroni, meat. They dreamed their dreams and discussed them as mere chimeras of the imagination, unrealizable, unattainable.

"As soon as this war is over, I'll run home and then straight to Righetto the baker and I'll eat two hundred cookies," one would say, his imagination and his hunger enlarging the capacity of his stomach.

"I'll do better than that," mocked a second, "I'll make it three hundred."

"Go on . . ." ridiculed a third, "why not make it a thousand?"

Day by day I discovered new tragedies.

Several years before a small family lived quietly and contentedly in the Abruzzi, a region known for its poets, its mountain landscapes, its rugged inhabitants. The father, mother, and a young son, still a boy, had a modest home there, a field and a cow. In the spring and in summer, the work of plowing and planting was done with assiduous care. In the wintertime, when so many hours had to be spent indoors, the three wove straw baskets and thus added to the family income. Life was plain, monotonous, yes, no distractions came to break the even tenor of it, but the family did not complain, they were satisfied. Now and then they took a trip, a short one to shop for necessities or to barter something superfluous for something needed. The boy attended the rural school and grew up as all children of his age grow up, more preoccupied with the building of a cage for the bird caught in the woods or with fishing for the brook trout than with doing his schoolwork.

Trouble had seldom touched the little home, except in a small way when it became necessary to incur a small debt in order to buy more grain for the wheat field. Yes, life there was serene.

Came the war. The father was not called to the colors in the beginning, for he was the only support of his family, but in the subsequent years his status was ignored and he was sent for and recruited for construction work in the fortifications then being built on high Alpine peaks, miles away from his family in the south of Italy. The mother and his child lived on alone, until their home was razed to the ground in an air raid. The cow was killed, they escaped.

They found a place in which to hide, but the war went inexorably on, the Allies landed in Sicily and started the northward advance. The usual evacuation order came, the usual migration, the blocking of the roads, the truck.

First destination Terra Gaia, the second and worse one, if possible, Cesano. The poor country woman, accustomed as she had been to the clear mountain air, to simple, nutritious food, to the meticulous cleanliness of the Abruzzi housewife, suffered the tortures of hell. For the sake of her child she tried to resign herself to the inevitable, hoping against hope that in the near future life as she had once known it might return.

A line of trucks drove up to the camp one morning, empty this time except for the German soldiers manning them and a petty officer giving sharp commands. The refugees stared and wondered. What was going to happen to them now? Where would they be sent?

Room had to be made for more human cattle. The soldiers had come to take as many as possible farther to the North. Rolls were called, men, women, children, were forced into the waiting trucks.

"Get in . . . hurry . . . no, you can't go back for anything . . . hurry . . . hurry . . ." Meek, dazed obedience.

The Abruzzi mother sat in her shed. She did not hear the name being called. A friend came after her. Trembling in anticipation of what was coming, she rushed out and asked one of the soldiers on guard. He motioned her to follow the others who had preceded her. She refused.

"My boy is out there . . . in the fields. Don't you understand? He is only a little boy . . . he needs his mother . . . just let me get him . . . it won't take me long to find him. . . . Mario . . . Mario . . ."

No answer. Mario was too far away to hear her.

Off went the caravan.

Mario played on for hours. At noon he returned and looked for his mother. No one told him what had happened. He searched, but nowhere was his search rewarded.

He asked, he wept. Someone tried to explain, but he could not understand. Why . . . why had his mother left him? She had never done that before. Faces glanced at him, but they were indifferent faces. His was too common a fate to cause any great excitement. What was a lost child more or less, when there were so many others, old, young, sick, dying?

Hours go by and Mario quiets down. Ten years old, alone, he makes up his mind. He will live by himself and for himself, forget. He locks his feelings tight within himself, plays by himself, eats his soup in a corner, refuses even to speak with anyone. The Allies come. Other boys and girls go off with their mothers. He watches them, then heads for Rome . . . alone.

The capital is crowded with children of all ages, all conditions of life. They have come from Sicily, Le Puglie, Abruzzi, the southern provinces liberated by the Americans. They are either in rags or clothed in discarded Allied uniforms. Eyes, brown, blue, green or black, but all of them sharp, wary, intelligent, searching.

Mario is lost in the great city. How can an ignorant country boy find friends? He suffers hunger, thirst, weariness. An American soldier finds him on a rainy night, sitting in a doorway, wet, shivering, and takes him with him. For two days he eats, then says good-bye in search of a change. He walks through a park and meets two other boys, alone, lost like himself. The three exchange formalities and he decides to join them. Ten years old, twelve, thirteen.

His companions know a lot more than he. They set to

work and teach him all the tricks of the new trade, if such it may be called. He learns how to look pitiful, how to make the passer-by feel sorry for him, how to steal a loaf of bread, how to carry a suitcase and perhaps run away with it, if the chance is given, how to get a free meal. At night when not wandering around, he sleeps in an abandoned box-car, in an empty house where the garden door can be easily opened. In a difficult contingency there is a convenient bridge with some protection from a too hot sun or too heavy a rain. Why worry?

A few months pass and the ten-year-old has acquired a new personality. Proficient in his methods, he now teaches others. It is not so bad, this life he is leading. There is food when he is hungry, he sleeps whenever he feels like it, he has money in his pocket, cigarettes are plentiful. Best of all he is his own boss. If he wants to smoke, he can do so without asking anyone's permission.

The indifference that surrounded him at the camp continues. True, he is often pushed around, he is insulted more than once, he is thrown out of many a place, but these things do not matter too much . . . there are compensations. . . .

The home in the Abruzzi mountains, the cow, the little cage he once built for the bird caught in the forest, his father, his mother . . . were they really true . . . or were they only a dream?

Toward the end of May the situation had grown worse hour by hour. The Germans tensed and the populations of Rome and of the surrounding areas, expecting liberation at any moment, broke out in sudden intemperate moves, in uncontrolled, too-evident satisfaction. The long-awaited coming of the Allies resulted into an often-critical analysis of the military operations that daily brought about new changes.

The Romans and the inhabitants of the surrounding regions saw the development of events from their own point of view. The delay in the Allied advance meant for them only prolonged suffering, more air raids, more hunger.

At the beginning of June, however, new signs were apparent in the anxious waiting. The feverish activity in air raids and artillery fire, in radio broadcasts, in war bulletins lacking in detailed accounts of any move by the German armed forces added rumors to the undercover news received surreptitiously over the clandestine radios and circulated in whispers and insinuations, indicating clearly that the stagnant atmosphere was lifting.

Not knowing how long I might be cut off from the capital, after its capture by the Allies, I decided on a hasty trip there.

The next morning I left in a truck directed toward the city. We drove for a while without meeting any trouble, but cannon fire made us come to a sudden stop. By some lucky chance we managed to get away and we continued on to Rome. I hurried through the business that had brought me there and made ready to return.

But the situation had changed hourly and it was not to be a simple task. News differed, one report often contradicting the one preceding it by a few minutes. Anxiety transpired in speech and glances, but it was an almost relieved anxiety, if such can be the case, the anxiety for the maturing of plans, nurtured for many months in the minds of old and young alike, longed for, prayed for, that the endless problems be solved once and for all. In spite of the fact that some fear for the safety of the capital tightened many a throat, its citizens felt that the arrival of the Allies would at least mean a definite improvement.

Until midnight I attempted the impossible in trying to get back to Castel Gandolfo. It was useless. No one was willing to take the chance of driving me there. I finally had to give up the idea, not without remorse at having left my charges in the Castelli, when my presence might have meant a great deal to them.

The next morning I was told that the Allies had entered Castel Gandolfo, also that the Germans had retreated to the flatlands below. Not knowing how long this state of affairs would continue and unwilling to wait, I decided to find a way of getting through the German lines. It was imperative that I reach the Castelli.

A taxi driver agreed to take me as far out of the city as, in his opinion, safety permitted. We discussed the point of whether to take the Old or the New Appian Way. It was our luck that we settled on the New, for, just then, on the Old Appian the American and German armies started exchanging heavy artillery fire.

I had hoped my driver's limit of safety meant that he would take me far on my way, but I was keenly disappointed. He stopped his machine only a few hundred yards from the Roman Gate through which he had taken me and said firmly that was as far as he would go. He explained that he had to take care of his own skin, that his family, his children were waiting at home and he could not let them down. I understood, got out, and started on foot. There was nothing else to be done. In Rome I had heard that the railroad bridge over the Appian Way had been destroyed.

I met few pedestrians. Rome at this point extends a number of miles beyond the gate. Stores locked and barred, a strange atmosphere hung over the neighborhood. Was it the hope of victory or a vision of possible defeat?

The Germans on the far side of a race track sat waiting in armored tanks and threw dark looks at me. I could not figure out whether they were surprised or astonished at my presence on that road. I recalled the way the German soldiers in the Anzio area had once looked at me, but there was a difference here, an uncertainty, an indecision.

No objections, however.

"Let us onward, for the long road doth drive us."

I kept on going and smiled to myself as I thought of the verse from Dante and figured the miles I still had to travel before reaching my destination.

The greater the distance from Rome, the more numerous the Germans. I left the beaten path and cut across the fields. Bad decision. While on the Appian Way the Germans had been sitting quietly in their tanks, here I found them in trenches.

And yet they let me by, none of them taking the trouble of bothering me. I reached a farmhouse, went in and out the back door. I headed for another not far away, and another. How long would I be able to play my little game? I was sure it could not last. How often had I found myself where the battle raged, where the dead lay around me too numerous to be counted, how many times had death stared me in the face! More than once I had admitted to myself that I might end up in rather bad shape, but on that day, on that road, I soon developed a feeling akin to resentment that I might perhaps lose my life when peace seemed to be in sight not only for me, but for thousands of others.

Back to the road again. It turned abruptly at one point. A group of houses prevented me from seeing what lay ahead. I rounded the curve and found myself looking at a line of heavy tanks. They stood there and they pointed toward Rome. I waited, not knowing how to proceed. Before I could make up my mind, the tanks veered unexpectedly and dashed off in the direction I was bound for . . . Albano!

"This really looks like a tank battle," I said to myself and streaked across the fields.

I had not gone far when I sighted a group of peasants, leaping madly about, waving their arms, yelling.

"We've made it! We've made it!" I heard.

I puzzled my head about the meaning of the words.

As I approached the group, someone shouted.

"They have come at last!"

"Who?" I questioned.

"The Americans."

"Where?"

"There! Look!"

It was really so. They were right. In front of me stood the same tanks I had seen a short while before at the curve in the road. I had taken them for German tanks, now, as I looked more closely, I recognized the American helmets.

They were with us! Grimy, eyes weary and red-rimmed from loss of sleep, shirts caked with mud and grease, sweaty, fagged out, they lolled by the side of the road, leaned against their tanks, crouched on a broken wall, the boys who had come from another world to make me happy on a sunny afternoon.

"Un Sacerdote," * a voice called out. I answered in English.

"American?" from another.

"No, Irish."

"Where did you come from?"

"From Rome."

They rushed at me then, amazed, grinning sheepishly, happy as youngsters, plied me with questions. Why this, why that . . . on and on.

One of them left the tank on which he had been leaning and joined the others. He knelt before me.

"Bless us, Father," he asked simply.

The sinking sun cast its soft radiance of crimson and gold. The Appian Way pointed onward, a glistening blade of steel slashing the green of the countryside. Peasant faces trembled with emotion as the youthful heads of the American boys bent to receive the blessing of God. I prayed for their safe return to America.

One of the lads had not moved from where he stood. He leaned against a tank, a child in his arms, caressing him, wordlessly, automatically, his gaze lost in space. Was

* A priest.

he thinking of his own little one at home, of the crosses scrawled at the end of his mother's letter received perhaps just the day before? He stood there thoughtful, dreaming his dream, the dream the same in the mind of any soldier of any land. A dream of returning home and soon to Robert, Mike, Hans, or Antonio. The child in his arms nibbled contentedly on a long-awaited chocolate bar.

My trip to Castel Gandolfo was rapidly accomplished . . . in an American jeep — Joe's jeep — that was placed at my disposal by the officer in charge. We tore up the hills, the trees flashed by, the fields disappeared one by one, the ruined houses did not look so hopeless. . . .

"We shall rise again . . . give us a little time . . . ," I thought I heard them whispering as we dashed along.

What was that? What was happening? The pealing of thousands of bells shut off all other sounds, the deep tones of huge bronze bells, the tinkle of others. The message, the same . . . thanksgiving . . .

Castel Gandolfo! My friends caught sight of me. I was surrounded by a shouting, weeping, praying, hysterical crowd. Hands were stretched out to me. I jumped out of the jeep . . . the bells pealed on. . . .

"Rome is liberated . . ."

"Not yet, but it is only a question of hours . . ."

"But then how did you get here?"

"I left the capital . . ." and I told the story of my escape. . . .

IV

THE LOST CHILDREN OF THE WAR

IV

THE LOST CHILDREN OF THE WAR

". . . They had no longer any wish for play . . . for anything . . . all they wanted was a miracle that might make them warm again . . ."

WITH THE ARRIVAL OF THE ALLIES IN ROME AND WITH their advance to the Gothic Line in the North, the existing problems were solved, or rather there seemed to be a good chance for their solution. But the liberation of the capital produced other problems far from simple. Among the most important was the repatriation and rehabilitation of the refugees who crammed the cities and the concentration camps.

I knew the problems well as I had had the full opportunity of following the saga of these unfortunates. Conditions were tragic, rendered more so by the refugees themselves. These people were anxious to go back to their native towns, to their small homes, to the fireplaces they had been forced to abandon.

The long lines of wanderers of months ago started once again. More tattered and torn than ever, worn, undernourished. They moved slowly, painfully toward the South from Rome in spite of orders by the Allied Command, which was doing its utmost to keep this exodus down to a minimum.

An old man, a very old man follows his small grandchild with feeble, halting steps. He holds in his hand a stringless guitar. He walks in silence. The little boy shoulders a long stick. At its end hangs an empty can, which with the aid of a bit of wire has been turned into some kind of crude cooking utensil. This is their only baggage. The two have only each other. The child's hair is matted. It has had no acquaintance with a comb for months. His father, a village clerk in one of the occupied zones, lost his life in Albania. His mother died of blood poisoning in a concentration camp.

I question the old grandfather. He answers me and his voice trembles.

"Is it possible that I, the oldest, must be the last one to die?" he queries at the end of our short talk.

Strange to say, there is a certain amount of gaiety in the air. There are women who can still sing, young girls who smile, and little children who are again learning how to play jokes on one another.

A car rolls by. The foot-weary travelers wave and shout their greetings and the riders shout and wave in return. Down the road, far down, home is waiting, home, hope, life. Every heart tends toward it to begin once more, to forget the past.

"I have lost my house and my furniture, everything. But as soon as my son returns from prison camp . . . there'll be enough of us to rebuild. . . ."

Most of them are from the Cassino region and each one knows that town and village and hamlet are gone.

"Who cares? I was born there and I want to die there," and they struggle on.

In Rome it was being said that there were at least a million refugees. In the first few weeks of the summer of 1944, many of these returned to their homes. Only those remained who had lived in Sicily and in other zones not easily accessible from the capital.

The refugees started out in high spirits, but upon arrival at their destination, they found only misery staring them in the face. Those especially who lived in the Casino and Frosinone regions were stunned to find nothing but scorched land, as the typical phrase well described the aftermath of the war.

To me this condition was, of course, familiar. I had traveled those roads so often. I remembered well the ruined houses, the burned-out forests, the villages wiped out, the absence of life.

And yet, before the war, these centers had been exuberant with life, the fields luxuriant. Each small plot of ground had been made use of, and the landscape had been green, filled with trees, vineyards, fruit groves.

Against the craggy rocks of the background, tall and gray and bare, the picture had been one not easily forgotten.

Now . . . hunger, thirst, sickness. No water, no electric light, no food, no clothing. All was gone and men and women and children felt lost, alone, abandoned, for the war was still going on and it was hardly possible to think of bringing aid to mere man.

At a time when civilization and technical progress were

at their highest, people lacked even the barest of necessities. Life had swung back to the cave era.

There was an abundant supply of unexploded mines, however, of bombs, of grenades, in village and road and hillside. Their invisible presence prohibited much activity of any kind.

The spectacle was terrifying. Skeleton houses rose stark against the blue. The streets had disappeared under piles of rubble, rocks, bricks . . . graveyards, unrecognizable as once-thriving communities. All power gone, all the logic of living.

This is what destruction lacks: logic.

Holes, here, there, everywhere, too many of them pools of swampy black water, gray-green foam floating on their surfaces. The only sound, the gloomy croaking of frogs.

Not an animal around. They might have been swallowed by the man-made earthquake.

From useless wooden poles hung the broken wires of world communication.

Life had been lived here? It seemed hard to grasp.

The province of Littoria had undergone a similar fate. This was the province that in years past had been redeemed, this the place where swamps had been turned into fertile fields. The Germans had knocked down the banks of the canals and reduced the whole area to its former status. It was now an immense boggy land.

Farmhouses built with so much care and labor lay half submerged in the slimy waters, the trees bent to show their discontent at finding themselves in such unusual surroundings.

Miles and miles of pestilential waters were anew the happy hunting ground of the mosquito, the deadly scourge of those regions. Nothing to stop the insidious work of the almost invisible foe lurking in every inch of water and in the grasses that stretched up and out for a breath of fresh air that was not there. Desolation and hopelessness!

And yet there, even there, the lost people went by the thousands. A few months later malaria broke out. From reports received, I learned that 30,000 people in the province of Frosinone were stricken by the dread disease.

One of the local doctors wrote:

"Malaria has invaded our province, has penetrated our homes. It is striking us hard. Whole families are ill. We see them in every house, we meet them on every road, white, weak, listless. In Zone —— once completely redeemed, and where malaria was only a faraway, sad memory, we have had 9,000 cases in the last four months."

Millions of mosquitoes breeding in the swampy region invaded the homes, if such they could be called, unprotected as they were from outside interference. No doors, empty windows, roofs caved in. What a paradise they found!

Thus did malaria complete the mowing down of the last shred of physical or moral endurance of whole populations, already reduced to a minimum of strength by lack of food and the fatigue of long, uninterrupted, weary journeys. In many towns it caused more harm, even, than the war.

"What's the use of trying to fight this battle?" men and women asked.

A certain spirit of fatalism began to be felt. I saw men

suddenly fall to the ground, shivering from fever, dragging themselves to the side of the road to lie there helpless and spent. Mothers unable to raise a hand from sheer weakness, watching their young ones with desperate eyes as the little ones begged for help.

When the children were stricken, hundreds of them died, unable to withstand the deadly disease, anæmic and badly nourished as they were.

On the heels of one of my many visits to the scourged areas, I set up an anti-malaria committee and invited a number of doctors and specialists to form part of it. The Vatican put at our disposal its valuable supply of quinine and, through the great interest shown by H. E. Myron Taylor, the Allied Command provided me with a great quantity of atabrine.

The doctors made a thorough examination of all the children in the afflicted zones and confirmed our fears that the majority of them had contracted the disease.

These examinations were often carried on under the wierdest of conditions and in the strangest of places. In one village, I recall, there was not a house standing. Only parts of walls, arms lifted up to heaven to shout their uselessness. The children huddled together out in the open. We had luckily found a space cleared of rubble. Some crouched on the ground, too far gone to stand. Their mothers awaited in silence the result of our work.

Teeth chattering in spite of the mild weather, the youngsters approached the doctor's table, fearful and anxious of the consequences.

Joe, about eight years of age, trembled more than the

others. Enormous eyes, thin to emaciation, belly big and swollen, he stood, watching, and waited his turn. As the doctor called him, he burst into tears and refused to move. He had to be lifted onto the table. The doctor proceeded with the examination and the weeping never ceased. In heavy silence, the others watched.

Four brothers followed Joe, aged from six to twelve, holding on tight to one another, afraid that this might mean another separation. They were orphans. Their parents had both died in an air raid.

Toward the end came a small tot as high as a grasshopper, brighter than the rest. Everyone looked at him and began to smile. No sooner was he on the table than he began to joke, make faces, and entertain the whole assemblage . . . a born clown. The heavy atmosphere lifted as if by magic.

We finished our work and started toward our next stop. The road was difficult to find as it led through fields gutted with holes.

Our car was a tiny Topolino (a small Fiat car, somewhat like an Austin). Soon we ran into trouble. To make matters worse it began to rain and night was not too far away.

On we jogged until suddenly . . . mud! Down we went, deep. The back wheels refused to budge. Now what? Where could we go? No one around, nothing. Only holes, mud, rain, and more clouds rushing across the sky toward us.

"Wish we could get a horse," said one.

"A horse . . . in this area?"

Gloom, darkness, solitude. What weight of silence! Where are those branches of trees that might help us get the car out and that must be lying around? Hard questions to answer.

We got out. A Topolino is supposed to be the lightest of cars. It had always seemed so to us. That night it weighed as much as a truck, loaded with guns.

For two whole hours we struggled. Two long hours with bare trees standing guard, knee deep in mud. Around us the field had turned into a swamp. The few branches we had been able to find cracked under the wheels.

At last, however, we won the battle. And at last we were on our way toward shelter and sleep.

Suddenly we burst out laughing. We had looked at one another and realized that our appearance was not of the best.

"Monsignor, you have mud even in your ears," one of my companions said.

In the fall of 1944, I witnessed more horror. No matter where I went, in a few moments my car would be surrounded by a crowd of people, pleading for medicine — men, women, and little ones, trembling and shaking.

Yet, amid all this desolation I thought I could see a spark of life. We saw group after group working in rubble and broken-down walls busily trying to rebuild what once had been a home. In a few months the work of reconstruction had taken a great step forward. And yet, even those who could be called the luckiest lived in pitiful circumstances.

In one town, a community of nuns could boast of only one room. Only one, as the whole building had been practically destroyed. Here in the midst of scattered, broken glass, the windows protected only by pieces of canvas, they lived

Young citizens begin the day's chores

Dairy Farmers provide milk for the towns

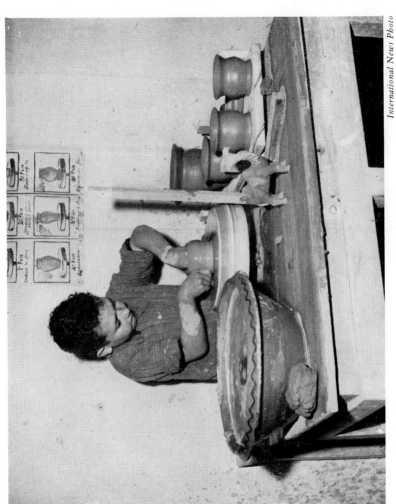

A potter in the making

No longer eating in the streets

. . . somehow. Whenever it rained, they crowded in a corner, where part of the roof still existed.

Nearby they had discovered a large abandoned barn, half of it in ruin. There they organized four classrooms and there the children went, attracted by the lunch distributed to them at noon, far more than by the love of learning.

One night I lay in my bed in a room on the ground floor of an old ramshackle place. The bed was an army cot with a mattress I could not say was soft. Neither could it be said that the room was full of the comforts of life. At the windows the usual canvas. No glass and the cold of mid-autumn blew in, whistling merrily around my ears. On the floor a number of tin cans gathered in the rain drop by drop as it came seeping through the ceiling.

Toward midnight it began to snow. The wind blew the thick flakes into the room, piled them high on the floor and around my bed. In spite of my blanket — I actually had one — the cold soon became unbearable. I could not sleep and I got busy trying to find the meaning of all this misery. To understand another's pain we must suffer. That had been said often. I thought of a line I had read from Veuillot's writings: "Certain things are not seen with understanding, unless with eyes that have known tears."

I was cold, but after all, my condition might still be an object for the envy of many. I had a bed, a mattress, a blanket. Best of all, the snow was not falling on my bed and the canvas did give a certain amount of protection. I really had a great deal, when I compared it with the children of Cassino.

These, thousands of them, not far from me still slept

under the open sky, or, if lucky, in a cave or among the stones piled around a space where the trees had been cleared by hard work, and often having eaten nothing except a bite of bread, and perhaps not even that. What about them? What about the thousands crowded in army barracks, drafty, wet, cold, where tuberculosis was rampant among the weak and undernourished? How many thousands? Who could tell? It was impossible to reach even a comparable figure. In the towns that had been destroyed there were no offices, no books, no tabulations. The individual had lost all identity, and life and death were no longer subject to the laws of statistics.

In November 1944, the first relief material — food and clothing — came from America, voluntary offerings gathered by the American Relief for Italy. This generous aid was particularly providential at the time, as an unusually cold winter added considerably to the hardships of the population.

Never will I forget the poignant scenes I witnessed that Christmas of 1944, while going from town to town distributing the first gifts of clothing from America to the children.

On December 22nd, we happened to be in a small village, Valmontone by name. It was a day bright with sunshine, but lashed by a cold, biting wind that made it difficult to breathe and froze our ears. Valmontone looked deserted, gray, dusty. Time and time again we had heard its name mentioned in the war bulletins. It lay as if passive in its squalor and poverty under the cold December sky.

We saw a few brave souls dragging away at stubborn rubble, searching hopelessly for what were to them the riches of the long ago. Each blow of the pickax marked a step toward another lost hope.

One house was still standing, slightly damaged, but there was not a single pane of glass in its windows. It had been assigned as a school.

The children were waiting for us. They had come alone or in groups of three or four, from caves in the hillside, from cellars, from no one knew where. Some were crying. All of them ragged, dirty, covered with lice, pale, anæmic, trembling and shaking, cold and feverish.

Did I say ragged? Some, many in fact, were clothed in wrapping paper, held together with wire! They sat together, close together, on a long bench, feet held high so as not to touch the icy coldness of the ground below them.

Naked in December! One small boy — Rocco was his name — was only seven! He was weeping bitterly. There was no room for him on the bench and his feet were almost frozen!

All of them were livid from the cold, eyes ringed in deep black circles. These were the small mischief-makers of yesterday! They had no longer any wish for play, no wish for anything, whether fun or frolic. All they wanted was some miracle that might make them warm again.

The miracle did happen. America had worked it.

"Here . . . and here, and here . . . yes . . . this is for you . . . all for you. Take this package . . . sweets . . . a bar of chocolate . . . a dress . . . a coat and a pair of shoes . . . yes, it's yours. . . ."

"Mine? All mine?"

"Yes. . . ."

"Do I put these shoes on?"

"Are they too big for you?"

"No . . . no."

And the child runs away, afraid it may not be true, holding onto his treasure.

Smiles, smiles at last! Smiles in payment for wool, for leather . . .

We watched him and the others and we felt happier than we had been for weeks. Happiness is often brought about by very small things.

The women wept more frequently now. During the war, they had borne the hardships of their lives with strength and resignation. Hope had still held sway in their hearts.

"My husband will return. . . ."

"My son will no longer sleep on the bare ground. . . ."

The war is over now. It may be going on somewhere else, but here it has ended. And yet anguish remains.

"What shall I do? I am alone. . . ."

Her son still sleeps on the bare ground. Her husband has not returned.

"If this goes on, my son will die."

They mourn for the children who have disappeared, the boys who have suddenly vanished, leaving no trace, no clue that might help in finding them.

Armies file by, tanks, endless columns of trucks, all wending their way toward the North. And boys of village and town follow them, lead by a beckoning mirage which for them spells food and life. It means adventure, bread, excitement, and the kindness of the soldier boy from Texas, and Tony's Neapolitan dialect. It holds out the forbidden fruit and they go.

The reason might have been loneliness, hunger, broken family ties. They hoped the soldier they followed might give them care, affection, an almost certain meal. The women — mothers, wives, sisters — struggle on, the boys go toward the unknown that holds out to them a ray of the sunlight that for so many weary months the world has denied them.

Christmas Day of 1944, I returned to Naples, so as to be present at the arrival of a number of ships bringing supplies from the A.R.I.

Along the way, we stopped the car and began to eat our lunch.

Across the road stood a small badly damaged cottage. It was high noon. The air blew cold and brisk. Two men and a woman came out of the cottage and walked toward the car. They asked us many questions, anxious to hear any news we might have to give them.

From them we learned plenty. In the country round-about, bands of boys, driven by hunger, had entered homes and held up the inhabitants for whatever they could get. They were always fully armed and their daring was beyond belief.

We heard that on the preceding day a number of them, from twelve to fifteen years of age, had succeeded in robbing the headquarters of the carabinieri and had escaped with a good supply of guns and ammunition. It sounded incredible, but we were told later it was true.

On the Appian Way it was a frequent occurrence to meet scores of these roaming youngsters, bound from the South of Italy toward the capital. During the conflict, they had learned all the tricks of their trade, as they helped in the fight against the German invaders. Now that the Germans were gone, hunger and want had become the enemy and had driven them to repeat past performances.

However, although many acts of vandalism were committed, by far the greater number of these lost children just sat and begged by the side of the roads, waiting, hoping that some kind driver of a jeep might come along, take pity on them, and give them a lift.

I had seen Naples after the liberation, but I had had little time at my disposal in which to form any definite opinion of the situation, or study its most serious aspects.

In that short space of time the number of wandering children had grown enormously. Naples could be called the meeting place for these youngsters from the South. Here they gathered and planned their exploits. These young adventurers, the *scugnizzi* of old, bright and intelligent, joined the *sciuscià*,* of today, ready for any work, any service useful to anyone and often dishonest.

Crowds of barefooted adolescents, wearing the most outlandish clothes, more often than not mere rags, the caps of every army in the world on their heads, were to be found anywhere and everywhere on the sidewalks, in front of barracks, offices, stores. Their favorite spot was the harbor.

In the Piazza Matteotti where headquarters of the Allied

---

* Italian version of "Shoeshine," the cry of the shoeshine boys of post-war Italy.

Command were situated and nearby, in the "Galleria," a place far from adequate for great crowds, it was a hopeless task to try to count them. They were all over the place, always carrying their "shoeshine" box and with clothes bulging with stolen goods. Some laughed, others wept, but all showed the unmistakable signs of malnutrition and disease.

Nothing was safe from these small human termites, who entered forbidden areas, stole everything on which they could lay their hands, useful or not, from automobile tires to uniforms, sheets, and cigarettes.

City Hall Square had been surrounded with barbed wire fences to protect the automobiles of the Allied Commands. Guards watched, standing where they could see every corner. In spite of them, the *sciuscià* succeeded in getting through and making away with car parts, unbreakable glass, clothing. . . .

A jeep stops in front of a door. A soldier gets out and goes through the door intent on his errand. He returns after a few minutes and one of the tires is gone from his car!

Comical incidents often occur.

A gang of boys stands guard on a deserted street. Hands in pockets, hats askew, they keep watch over a young colored American G.I. lying in drunken stupor at the curb, probably a victim of the poisonous liquor then on sale.

A second group of boys makes its appearance.

"Who's that?" one of the new arrivals asks.

"He belongs to us," is the astonishing reply.

"How come?"

"We paid for him . . . two thousand lire . . . want him?"

"Sure . . . how much?"

"Three thousand. . . ."

The bargain is concluded. The new owners take up the watch waiting for the third customer.

They walked through the Galleria offering their wares: chewing gum, cigarettes, a pair of shoes. Some of them had little luck and, after long hours of effort, they were exhausted, white, and spent. Then the older ones, the huskier ones came to their aid, in a spirit of solidarity and charity that is probably not so frequently found among adults. They took care of the small fry, fed them, worked harder in order to give them the necessary bread to sustain life. Each small gang worked alone, sometimes fought one another, but when it happened that a battle had to be fought against big odds, against big fellows, then they joined together and usually won.

The harbor of Naples was their favorite field, the goal of their ambitions. Here came the wealth, from overseas. No guards, no barbed wire, no fences, not even electrically charged wires could keep them away, or back the invading tide of the young desperadoes, battling alone in a world that to them spelled only tragedy.

The emotions of the past years had piled up in their hearts and bodies during the bombardments, the food rationing, the death in their families, the breaking-up of close ties, and exploded. In the breakdown of social values, in a new vision of what life might be, the emotions of the period of terror rose to the surface and recognized no restraint.

After all, it must be remembered that in the not far

distant past, the radio itself had incited the citizens of town and city to sabotage, to the procurement by any means at hand of material needed for the war effort. At that time the risk had been taken and surmounted, the success of the enterprises had meant not only personal satisfaction, but also prizes and praise.

In Rome, during the German occupation, I happened to be crossing a bridge over the Tiber when I noticed a German truck stop just across the river from where I stood. A soldier stepped out and walked over to a fountain for a drink. Three boys suddenly appeared out of somewhere and with monkeylike movements, faster than my eye could follow them, they clambered up the sides of the truck, stole several tools and spare parts, and disappeared in a flash. The soldier fired after them, but to no earthly use. The boys safely carried away their contribution toward the resistance movement with no thought of personal gain.

In Naples, in 1944, from the point of view of these boys, conditions had not changed. There was among other things such an abundance of supplies, such a waste, that temptation was too hard to resist. There was hunger, the hunger of years of want. The indifference of well-fed, well-dressed, well-cared-for people exasperated them. And besides it was so easy to get a package of cigarettes or two tin cans of meat!

"There are so many! Why is it wrong to take a few?" they wanted to know.

The war was over, but suffering for them was still present and to a greater degree. So many chances had to be taken in order to obtain even a little of all that was needed! How often had a small twelve-year-old Neapolitan returned home at night, tears in his eyes because he had been unable to bring home to his sick mother even a piece of bread or a bottle of medicine that she needed so much!

The majority of those who could still boast of a home kept religiously in their hearts the love of their own firesides. The family tie was strong, although on the surface it seemed as if anything with any value had been suppressed.

Life was tough. It was difficult to pay too much attention to conventions, and the actions of adults offered such bad example! More often than not the children were taken advantage of by the latter, who, by the output of a few pennies here and there, obtained riches worth thousands of lire. This commerce was also given fuel by the Allied soldiers. The *sciusciá* with his practical common sense and an inborn feeling for business was the go-between in the marketing of cigarettes, mechanical devices, foodstuffs. Often the merchandise that changed hands was considerable.

The great harbor of Naples was unrecognizable. The boats, gray, camouflaged, dramatic, stopped at the broken-down piers. Cases, boxes, bales of merchandise of all kinds were unloaded and piled high. The port area took on the appearance of a fort under guard, surrounded by barbed wire, alive with soldiers, guns ready to point at any unwary intruder.

Tireless in their efforts, the M.P.'s did their utmost, but they did not seem able to discover how the impossible had been accomplished. A boat was unloaded and on the morrow much of the merchandise had vanished!

Captain Chaplin of the port police was frankly worried at the turn of events. The merchandise kept on disappearing. He and I often discussed the situation at night when we met in a room of the Caetani Palace.

During my second visit to Naples, I was the guest of an American colonel who lived at the palace. At night we met and spoke of the existing problems, and particularly of the widening corruption, trying to formulate an answer to the many questions all responsible elements were asking.

The colonel as well as the captain considered the situation not only from the point of view of military security, but also from its human aspect. It began to look as if the authorities were utterly helpless to cope with the situation.

Whole families were organized, headed by small demons who gave orders and handed out jobs to their parents and relatives.

A family of five, a father and his four children, three boys and a girl lived in one of the old narrow, crooked streets, alleys to call them by a more correct name, of which there are so many in Naples. Utter neglect and the absence of any work done by the now defunct street cleaning department had brought about a condition of unbelievable squalor.

The place where the family lived could not by any stretch of the imagination be called an apartment. It was in the cellar of an old building, access to it down a couple of steps from the street. Sparsely furnished with pieces that might have seen better days, it spoke of wretchedness and neglect. The faces of the occupants matched the surroundings.

In front of the house, across the street, stood a fish store, where the owner fried fish from morning till night and poisoned the air with the rancid oil he used. Two doors away was the home of the old shrew of the street, the one who knew everybody, was familiar with everybody's business, who gave advice and predicted the future to young and old. They called her the "Capera." The name had clung to her from the old days, when she went from house to house combing the women's thick, shiny black hair.

The father worked as a waiter, but earned little or nothing. One son and a daughter managed to bring in a few lire. Life became harder each day.

But now the Allies have come, and with them life brightens. Tony, the ten-year-old member of the family, has his wits about him. He is a bright, intelligent child. The Americans take a fancy to him and to his six-year-old sister, Nunziata, whom he always drags along for sympathy. Soon after, bread and corned beef find their way into the house.

Days go by and Tony formulates a plan of his own. He has a number of friends and their pockets are always filled with thousand-lire bills. He must branch out in business if he is to keep up with them.

He borrows a boat from his uncle Gaetano the boatman, and rows out into the bay. Nunziata accompanies him.

The American sailors are very fond of the big Italian pistols. In exchange for them they give away mountains of food. Tony knows of a toy store that manufactures toy pistols that look very much like the real thing. At a distance, from the deck of a boat, for instance, who can tell the difference between a toy pistol and a real one? Not the sailor boy. He is easily fooled.

"Food first, then pistols."

The bargain is concluded. Tony returns.

On another day, Tony again has a bright idea.

"May I come aboard?" he calls up at one of the sailors leaning over the rail of a ship anchored far out in the bay.

The sailor laughs and nods. Tony climbs, small sister close at his heels.

For ten days they live on the boat, away from Naples, stuffing themselves with food. Tony even tries smoking, but he is not too fond of it. He does it only to give himself airs.

Life on the boat also means work for Tony. At the end of his stay, he has learned all he wants to know about ships: where the portholes lead, where the food and the supplies are stored, how to get in and out of a ship with ease and expediency.

Well-fed and well-informed, Tony and Nunziata return home, pockets stuffed with provisions, hands filled with gifts from the friends they have made on the ship.

The operation is repeated again and again and, each time, Tony and little sister return home with whatever is needed. The father, the older brother and sister, the "Capera" join forces, and as if by magic the miserable hovel is transformed into a storehouse for the food and the variety of merchandise transferred from the well-stocked holds of the Liberty ships.

At first the father and his eldest son are afraid, but Tony allays their fears and urges them to continue their efforts.

The "Capera" with her boasted faculty of seeing into the future predicts villas and palaces.

Tony is happy and gay now. Everyone at home is eating his fill and for a time, at least, there is no thought, no worry of the morrow. He thinks himself a hero who has won his battle against big odds.

He has that Neapolitan trait, made up of big words and big deeds, that often hides deep and noble sentiments. His beloved little sister is never away from him and she always enjoys the best gifts, the sweetest treats.

"Nunziata first . . . ," he says every time someone offers him anything.

He never forgets to hide her in a safe spot, whenever he has to go on a particularly hazardous mission.

And so Tony takes the place of his father, becomes as it were the head of the household.

But effort must be redoubled. Too many are beginning to help themselves at the supply from overseas.

Tony gets more notions. He follows the soldiers, talks to them, suggests, and a new business is on the way. The soldiers send him on errands, more or less honest, the "Capera" advises, and now he can carry on, in the harbor, on the streets, in and out of houses, wherever he pleases.

"No, Papa, you can't come along. You would only be in the way." The small son has become the mentor of the older man. He well understands that his father's mentality is not suited to the new atmosphere in which he works.

It may be difficult to understand, but it is nevertheless true, that these families, although existing through shady, unlawful means, were not really evil. Some became degenerated, true, in others destructive germs took root, but on the whole there was still real goodness in Naples.

The *sciuscià* who stole, who participated in illicit operations, who sold goods on the black market, who organized a wave of general thievery on the day of the armistice, taking advantage of the drunkenness en masse, who played on the good nature of the boy from Kentucky, did it only because he was hungry, better because those he loved were hungry. This, in his opinion, obliterated all scruples.

"What . . . must I die of hunger?" said one of them to me one day.

Besides, he loved adventure, he loved taking chances, daring was his favorite sport. In this new life, he tasted to the full the boundless freedom he found, and thoroughly enjoyed the triumph of putting something over on those who were older than he, on the rich, on the powerful, on the conquerors.

Once, not too far back, during the bloody "Five days" of Naples, he had helped set the mines that blew up the German tanks; he had scuttled through the streets of the city, had crept under barbed wire, or had dashed from a rain of machine-gun shells to find water for his sick mother "who was so thirsty"; he had climbed atop the roofs of high buildings to hurl the heavy tiles down on those hated steel helmets. Compared to all those adventures, getting a ride on Freddie's jeep was only a joke!

Many times I stopped to talk with one or another of these youngsters. They were cordial, talkative, unafraid to speak of their deeds, but, deep within them, I sensed a feeling of cynicism and distrust. Cynicism, for too early in life they had come in contact with horror and misery. Distrust, because, in any adult they met, they thought they found a potential enemy, a powerful one who could hurt them, who could deprive them of their hard-won liberty.

And the problem grew. It could be compared to an epidemic spreading its toxin slowly, inexorably, amidst a gunshot, a pinch of cocaine, a holdup and worse.

A realization of what was going on beat its hammer blows on the minds of those who visualized it as a river of unbridled passions rising steadily and finally overflowing its banks. They worried at the sight of the destruction of ideals and traditions handed down through the centuries, at the growth of a new and pitiful way of life.

The Allies had a deep comprehension of the children and their mischievous ways. The G.I.'s in general have left behind them grateful memories of the affection they poured upon the youngsters, the attention they showered upon them. They knew how to forgive their pranks, they enjoyed themselves at the sight of the natural outburst of gaiety that suddenly rose to the surface in those small friends they had made. Big boys themselves, far away from their own loved ones, they found in the *sciuscià* a younger brother, a small son. Whole days at a time they took them along, sharing their food with them, their cigarettes, their money. It was a common sight to see a G.I. seated in the midst of a crowd of children, laughing, joking, munching away at a bar of chocolate, a piece of candy, an apple and what not.

Officers also made friends of the *sciuscià*.

A general leaves his headquarters and a dark-skinned boy, poorly clad, flashes a bright smile at him as he opens the door of the car waiting at the curb, adding a salute, and a bow as if to the manner born.

The general notices him, smiles in return, steps into the car and off he goes to his destination, the Club.

As the machine comes to a stop, out pops the same boy from no one knows where, opens the door, smiles and bows. Surprised, the general smiles again, ruffles the curly head raised toward him, and gives an order to his aide.

"See that he gets a good lunch. He looks as if he needed it."

The episode is repeated a second day, a third. At the end of the third day, the general is moved by the perseverance of the boy who clings to the back of the car and follows him everywhere, ready to open the door with a smile and a bow.

Patsy is rewarded with a sailor's uniform cut to size, complete to the last detail. He reports at all conferences held by his idol and behaves like a perfect gentleman. He does not touch the liqueurs, but he stuffs himself with sweets, not too many for fear of a bellyache, and he sends home to his older brother and sisters the enormous packages of food, cigarettes, sewing needles and soap, that his friends, the sailors, give him.

"Monsignor, all Lux and Palmolive soap . . . two hundred lire a cake. My sister, Assunta, sold them for that much. . . . Gee!" he said to me one day.

The general leaves for America, gives him something for his family, and Patsy returns to his shoeshine box. Not all of these boys, however, acquired a general as a protector, or a fairy godfather. And, as often happens among the homeless, many were more lonely and in a worse state of abandonment than others.

In the palace, under the high, frescoed ceiling, where at night I slept in a huge room, I was assailed by the thought, the necessity of finding some way, some means of helping these poor little brothers of mine.

The spacious room, badly lighted, furnished with antique, moth-eaten pieces did not invite particularly pleasant thoughts. Besides, how could such thoughts germinate after a day in which the best sight I had seen had been that of a boy sitting on the steps of a church, biting into a piece of dry bread, tears coursing down sunken cheeks because his uncle had taken from him a can of pork and beans? I watched the painted canvas hanging from the ceiling swell in the wind like the sail of a ship and kept on thinking.

In that ancient room I relived my night in the broken-down house in Cassino, when the snow had drifted in and piled high around my bed. I recalled the caves and the cellars, the only shelters of so much humanity.

The officer in charge of the harbor police told me a story a few nights later.

The night was dark. Naples slept, guarded by the sentinels of the anti-aircraft observatories.

On the water close to the harbor, there is an unusual murmur of voices, subdued whisperings:

"Did you get in?"

"Yes."

"Does it float?"

"Sure."

The heads of the two boys appear within a black ring

floating on the waves. Then their shoulders, arms, hands.
They start to paddle, using slats of wood from broken boxes.
The black ring moves. It had been an empty gasoline drum.
Now it had turned into a boat.

Thus it was discovered how the merchandise lying
around on the piers kept vanishing, stolen by small ghostly
figures that had not been noticed for a long time, until one
night someone caught sight of the pairs of bright eyes peek-
ing out of each of a number of floating black rings! No wonder that barbed or electrically charged wire had been useless in preventing the mysterious disappearances.

We had long discussions one evening at the Caetani
Palace. It just happened that it was a special evening.
Christmas!

A certain aura of homesickness hung in the air, dampen-
ing the gaiety of the moment. It was reflected in the words
of the men, who spoke of their families, their faraway home-
lands, of old times, the traditional family trees, the gifts,
the happiness of children shouting their surprise at what
Santa had brought them. Some spoke reverently of the
religious character of the holy day. Faraway thoughts that
took on special meaning in the atmosphere in which we
were living.

Packages, gifts, cakes, cookies had come from across the
seas to enliven our spirits. We chatted and exchanged
views. Captain Chaplin told of the newest feats of the small
vagabonds and on that note our conversation widened to
include the appalling contrasts in the way of life.

Our room was warm, outside on the square a bitter cold
wind blew. We sat around a huge crackling fire. Most of

the fireplaces in Naples were cold and dead and on the sidewalks of the streets outside boys lay huddled together against icy walls in a hopeless effort to find a little warmth.

Something had to be done for these boys. That was obvious. But how and by whom?

The government? How could the government of Italy give any real attention to this problem, when so many other vital ones had to be dealt with, day after day, hour after hour? The whole of Italy was starving, millions of refugees were scattered, vast territories had been rendered uninhabitable by buried mines. Miles of fertile lands had been changed into malaria-infested swamps. Hospitals, homes were completely ruined or partly so. The cases of tuberculosis were growing to alarming proportions. And, with it all, no railroads, no mail, no telegraph, no ships . . . unless we counted the ones lying sunk at the bottom of the sea.

The Allies? The war was not yet over and any means offered to this work would be detrimental to the war effort. A great deal had been done. Two hundred grams of bread and much food was being distributed daily and this entailed not only expense, but tremendous organization. The Allies could not possibly do more for the time being.

The colonel, a man with a quick tongue and an ever-ready joke, always found a way of giving his opinion.

"What I would like to know is this," he remarked, "what is an Irishman doing here if he can't solve a simple problem like this?"

His words, said as a joke, held a spark of truth. I felt that each one of us had a great obligation, even if in a limited way, to save the children. I determined to do whatever lay in my power, to spare the little ones greater tragedies, to bring back into their hearts and souls a knowledge of kindness, hope, and love.

With this thought to guide me, I returned to Rome. What could be done? The important thing was to start.

Time worked against me. The American Relief for Italy took up a great deal of my day. I was also president of the Italian Medical Commission for the distribution of medical aid. My offices were crammed with thousands of people, mothers with husbands and sons in foreign prisoner-of-war camps, Jews patiently and unavailingly seeking news of dear ones, homeless children, men out of work. As director of Papal Medical Relief, I was in charge of a vast network of medical dispensaries, while new centers were daily being set up: dispensaries for children suffering from vitamin deficiencies, centers for the cure of pernicious anæmia, for diabetes, for heart diseases, and centers for the battle against malaria.

It was useless for me to think that I could, at least for the moment, dedicate myself directly to the care of the children.

My first thought was to mobilize all available energies, such as existing institutions, in tackling the problem. During the course of my work, I had close contact with hundreds of orphanages throughout Italy. I wrote to them or had collaborators call on them to discuss the possibility of their opening their doors to a large number of children, so as to take as many as possible of the wandering children from the streets.

"In the conditions under which we are working at present, we might be able to take in more boys. The trouble, however, lies in the fact that we do not have a place for them to sleep," wrote the head of one of the Institutions.

"We have plenty of room," wrote the director of another, "but we have no beds, no mattresses, no blankets."

"The great obstacle is the lack of food," concluded a third.

I noticed how each letter spoke of a different need. This carried the possibility of doing something concrete toward solving the problems of each one. All I had to do was to find and send to each locality whatever was missing and the lack of which prevented the Home from accepting more children.

It became apparent that a group of people would have to volunteer to seek out, to obtain, and finally to distribute the necessary items to each Institute.

Thus came into being the "Opera del Ragazzo della Strada" (Foundation for Homeless Boys).

The beginning had to be small. It was useless to look for new relief goods. Such foreign agencies as might have similar material would already have formed their own plan for distributing it.

I knew, however, that a great number of bales that had been brought from America had been ruined in the holds of the ships that had been flooded by war actions during the voyages. I asked the Italian National Agency for the redistribution of these discarded and moldy bales of clothing. Hospitals that had bought new beds before the war brought up the old rusty ones from the basements. Other beds were sent to us by the fire department; old broken-down cots by the army; and kitchen utensils, old cups, saucers, and plates were obtained from the Swiss Relief Agency, which had collected them in a house-to-house canvas. Later on, as the American Red Cross dismantled its Army Clubs, it turned over to us abundant equipment.

Our storehouses slowly filled with moldy clothes, rags, dishes, cups, bowls of all sizes and shapes, broken down beds, cots. There were a lot of shoes, but they all needed repairing and it was not easy to find a matching pair.

As the offerings came, the work of selecting, remaking, mending, cleaning went on unceasingly.

The beds were repaired and varnished, the canvas of the cots changed, the thousands of pieces of clothing, washed, taken apart, cut to a new measurement and made over.

Buttons by the hundreds were cleaned and sorted. Burlap bags were carefully pulled apart thread by thread and knitted into socks and stockings. Tables and chairs and chests were submitted to a process of rejuvenation. In the workrooms men and women busied themselves making coats and suits and trousers. Clothing for more than twenty thousand boys was the result.

There was great need of wool. To a Committee of Women we gave the task of collecting any and every oddment of old wool, fit only for the rag bag. They succeeded so well that ten thousand sweaters came out of our workrooms, after the wool had been unraveled, rewound, and knitted.

Sisters were in charge in workroom and storeroom and worked with zeal and amazing speed. My old friends from the Hospital of Monserrato gave of their time and their help at our offices, free of charge. The lawyer and the trolley-car motorman, the state employee and the banker pledged four and five hours work a day and they reported to us faithfully after their day's work was done. Institutes that took care of the washing and sewing of wearing apparel were the only group offered any payment and this only under the guise of food for those they sheltered.* The food we obtained came principally from American Relief for Italy, Inc., which also guaranteed a daily ration of milk to one hundred and eighty thousand children.

The close collaboration of rich and poor accomplished an astounding miracle of charity and brotherly love.

Our work did not keep us locked in an office. In order to organize the whole into a unit, we traveled throughout Italy four days a week, from the northernmost region to the most distant tip of Sicily. Everywhere we went, we visited hundreds of Institutes and hospitals.

In every town, we came in contact with children and more children. I had plenty of opportunity for studying the problem in its local and general aspect.

Rome had its own particular problem, because of the mixed character of its youthful population. A crowd of youngsters had poured into the center from the outlying slum suburbs, adding their number to that of the children of the evacuees who had come to Rome in the hundreds of thousands and the boys who had followed on the heels of the Allied armies.

Here, as in the southern cities, these boys were well

* As statistical information, during the first year of its life, "L'Opera del Ragazzo della Strada" was able to distribute 190,000 pieces of clothing, 258,000 sheets, blankets, and towels, 22,000 beds and pieces of furniture, and about 7,000 tons of foodstuffs.

trained in the art of jumping onto military trucks and at regular intervals pushing off some of the bales and boxes and bags they carried. They knew the ways of black-market procedure, of illicit trading. They organized themselves into gangs and robbed homes and market places.

Groups of them were easily distinguishable in the crowded areas, such as the railroad stations and the shopping districts. These places had been well chosen, for the Allied soldiers frequented them in great numbers. The railroad station, with its freight trains, provided them with booty aplenty and at night the empty cars gave them shelter.

In the larger squares, favorite spots for the black market, it was not difficult to obtain almost anything. Cigarettes, soap, razor blades, anything!

The root of the evil lay not so much in their own initiative as in the power of an organization, directed by a group of adults who ran few risks but took full advantage of the misery of these youngsters.

Although living these adventurous lives, the children were still not wholly lost. Under their hard shells, often fictitious ones, beat hearts that were still clean and that could be reached. However, it was easy to see that unless it were possible to tear them from the life they led they would soon be entirely corrupted.

I met one of them in the courtyard of St. Damascus in the Vatican one day. As I came out of the Palace, I noticed him talking with my chauffeur. He was about fourteen, not very tall for his age and, as he talked, he had a faraway look in his eyes. Compared to many others I had met, he was fairly well dressed, although his jacket was shabby and his shoes were too large for his feet. I listened to the story. At first he spoke haltingly, but then the words began to come out like a flowing stream. I wondered how many times he had had to repeat his story in the last few weeks. His account was full, detailed, anticipating all questions.

"I was born in Ethiopia and we lived happily together, my father, my mother, and I. Addis Ababa was my native town. Once in a while we went to a show. School wasn't bad. I had a lot of friends there and we had fun. We used to play in the clean, white yard of the school. . . ."

Then the war had struck. Bombs fell on his home. In the small cottage in the midst of the shattered new furniture lay the bodies of his father and mother.

He spoke more slowly now, stopping now and again as if to swallow the knot in his throat.

In 1942 he was brought to Italy from Africa with other Italian refugees. He traveled alone and he was alone on the pier, at Naples, where no one came to meet him.

The law required everyone to be searched. In his pocket, the guards found a letter an Englishman in Africa had asked him to mail in Italy. It was addressed to a friend of his.

The boy protested his innocence, his complete ignorance of what the letter might contain.

"I didn't know . . . I didn't know," I kept telling them, "but they wouldn't believe me."

Dazed by the strange accusations, he wept and pleaded. He was not believed and was sent to the North to a concentration camp. He was eleven, the others with him were much, much older. In solitude he learned hard lessons. At the camp, everyone was too busy to stretch out a hand in sympathy to a lonely child.

In 1943 — he was twelve then — they sent him, along with grown men, to work on the defenses of the Brenner Pass. For the first time in his short life, he experienced the bitterness of cold weather, the biting cold of the Alps that crept into his body accustomed to the warm sun of Africa. His young hands became callous, his arms ached, his feet tore and bled, as he mixed cement with a long-handled tool or made trip after trip carrying the hod filled with stones on his thin shoulders.

Months passed. Each day he grew more worn, thinner, weaker, but the hardships and the work never ended.

The Allies came. An American officer questioned him. Amazement grew in the officer's eyes as he heard the boy's story.

"But I have an aunt living in Rome."

"Is this really so?"

"Yes, here's her name."

The officer was finally persuaded and the boy left for the capital after a short wait.

While waiting he ate, he rested at last. No more work. Summer came and even on the Alps the cold was gone. Life had improved a lot.

The trip on the jeep is a great adventure. The thought of Rome, a home, and an aunt who will surely take good care of him, makes him laugh and joke. The soldiers also are good to him.

"And what will you do there?"

"Work, I guess — I'm used to it you know . . . but

I'll make money now . . . and I'll pay for my keep. . . ."

But in Rome no one knew of his aunt.

"Go to the Vatican. There's an information office, where you'll find out what you want."

No luck there either. He had just left its doors when I met him.

As he finished his story, I noticed that my chauffeur had opened the door of the car, reasonably certain that he would have another passenger.

The lad stayed with me several days, until I succeeded in finding a home for him. He spent most of the time in my office, his hands on my desk and his chin resting on his hands. Sometimes he followed with interest everything that I was doing. Suddenly a faraway look would come into his eyes and he would be a thousand miles distant. The lost look had gone, but I seemed to catch both a longing and a wish for something of his own — a home, a mother, a father, only a little of what any human heart desires.

This was one case. Like it there were a host of others, some even worse. By mere chance this lad had not had time to come in contact with the worst evil of the street.

But, as I have said before, although condemned and vilified, the children were not delinquents. Abandoned by men, they were not abandoned by the Almighty and, under the influence of His Grace, they taught us more than one lesson and furnished us with examples of charity and brotherly love, unique and memorable in an era of so much horror.

Sandro was an orphan, his parents buried under the ruins of Cassino. He lived in Rome with his small friends and sold cigarettes, shined shoes for the Allied soldiers under the porticoes of the Piazza Esedra. He got along, and at night, after he had eaten, he even had some money left over. Most of this soon went to the youngsters less fortunate or less able than himself.

One unlucky day he was run over by a jeep racing through one of the streets. He was taken to the hospital by a passer-by. It was necessary to amputate one of his feet, crushed under the wheels.

He had to stay in the hospital for two long months, but he was practically never alone. His friends took turns in visiting him and one of them at least was always at his bed-side keeping him company. Many a time the night nurse, coming on duty, would find a ragged *sciusciá* fast asleep by the bedside and would have to shake him firmly before he would be sufficiently awake to realize that it was time to leave. And his friends never came empty-handed. They brought him chocolate bars, chewing gum, hard candy, a piece of white bread, a pair of new trousers for the day when he would rejoin them.

The day he was dismissed, five of his small companions were waiting for him on the sidewalk in front of the hospital door. They looked sheepishly at the empty trouser leg and at the awkward crutch under his arm.

Sandro made a crude attempt at a joke. It sufficed, how-ever. They all laughed and made a great show of helping him along to the hovel where they had found a bed for him.

It was only a cot in the corner of a filthy room, but it was better than nothing. Every day one of them came to ac-company him toward the station. If it was not raining, Sandro would pass the whole day in the open lying next to Michael's shoeshine box near the entrance to the Grand Hotel. Michael became proud of him. Sandro was a distinct asset to his business. If one of the customers, moved by pity, asked for Sandro's story, it had by now been elaborated into an exciting account guaranteed to move anyone to tears. Sandro also at the end of the day felt he had earned the money Michael gave him.

Ever since his accident, Sandro had been thinking of an older brother that he had not seen for many months, but whom he knew was somewhere in Rome. Word went around among his friends and after a few weeks of intense search, they discovered him and brought him to Sandro's room as a surprise, one rainy afternoon.

That was a gay day in spite of gray clouds. What a feast they had! Canned meat, orange marmalade, and even a bottle of the worst possible wine!

The adults who shunned them like the plague could have learned many a lesson from these shoeshine boys. But instead, they ran from them, hurried past them on the street, as though the very sight of them was a humiliating reminder of their incapacity to help, or ignored them completely, accepting them unreflectingly as one of the strange phenomena in which they could not possibly have any personal interest.

Some writers depicted in the lives of the *sciuscià* only the side that humiliated the personality of the child and gave their impression that their occupation offered no other aspect than one of servile abjection. They did not understand or did not want to understand that many of these youngsters valued their work as an honest effort toward survival. A certain sense of pride upheld them, they refused to steal, they found in work their only means of keeping alive.

Beppe was one of these.

While playing in front of his home on July 10, 1943, he did not know the day would be a turning point in his life. Yes . . . the same thing . . . an air raid. Most of the people in the street or within the houses escaped. At the first sound of the sirens they ran to the shelters.

Beppe was small. He just stood where he was, too scared to move. All that he could do was to throw himself on the ground and cover his ears with his hands.

When it was over and he dared to lift up his head to look at the place, it was a shambles. Frightened out of his wits, he disappeared somewhere. He had seen his house demolished, he was sure his mother and father were buried under the ruins.

All day he wandered around Rome. Late that night a young woman found him weeping on a corner and took him home with her. He was happy for a few months and came to think of her as his own dear mother. A few months and the Germans came. They invaded the apartment building where he lived, rounded up some of the men hiding there and, by some strange confusion, took him with them and sent him off to Germany.

For two years he lived in the concentration camp. A priest there . . . also an inmate . . . took an interest in him, gave him lessons, and at the conclusion of the war saw to it that he was sent back as soon as possible to Italy.

Rome! At last he was there again after long, weary jour-

neys in cattle cars, after continuous changes from one house
to another, from one camp to a worse one, after undergoing
hunger, thirst, almost unbearable cold, after listening to
the crack of bombs falling around him, the shrieks of sirens,
the roar of tanks advancing across defeated Germany.

He had seen whole populations evacuated, thousands of
dead on battlefields and city streets, but through all those
months of torment, one idea had stayed fixed in his mind:
to find once again that peaceful corner he had been forced
to leave, for no understandable reason that he could see,
the humble home of his benefactress.

As soon as he reached Rome, he went to the family address and waited, sitting on the dark stone staircase, until
she came back from her work, fumbling in her bag for her
key. She was overjoyed to see him and fussed over him
while he washed and dressed.

He was older now and not only in years. He soon realized
that his foster mother was not rolling in wealth. He must
find a job and help to keep the home. He began to go from
one shop to another in the neighborhood looking for work.

So one day *sfilatino* (the name given to the long thin loaves
of Italian bread) came into being. It was the name they
gave him at the bar and grill where he had found a job.

"You have to have an identity card," someone told him.

He reported to the office where he had been sent.

"Name . . . first . . . last . . . father . . . mother . . . ?"

The clerk searches through the card index, comes back
with the address.

"Why did you say your father and mother were dead?

Here I find them registered in the refugee camp in Viale del Re."

"But my family was killed . . . I saw a bomb fall on the house. . . ."

"Not according to the information in these books . . . next . . ."

Sfilatino returns to the shop where he works and wonders what to do. He hesitates about going to the camp for fear of too great a disappointment. He is sure that his parents are dead.

Finally an idea strikes him. He writes his mother and addresses it.

"Is it true that you are alive, Mother? I found it out today. I am at Gallo's *rosticceria*."

The next day the letter is delivered. Twenty minutes later mother and son are together again.

"Beppe . . . Beppe . . . you are alive. . . ."

Before the owner of the *rosticceria* and the waiters looking on with unbelieving eyes, the two cling to each other.

In the fall I petitioned His Holiness, Pope Pius XII, to grant an audience to the homeless boys who frequented the many shelters scattered around the city. The Holy Father who among his many activities had always kept in his heart a very special corner for the stricken children of the war, consented immediately.

October 28, 1945, was "Sciuscià Day" at the Vatican. A famous date this, for in previous years, it had seen martial parades, columns of marching men, row upon row of cannon. By a strange coincidence on that same day, the year that had seen the so-called ending of World War II, a group of small war victims, ragged and unkempt, met in audience before His Holiness.

How many? It was impossible for us to count them. By previous arrangement about two thousand were taken to the Vatican by trolley cars. An innumerable number, however, came and kept coming.

In the Great Square of St. Peter the crowd of youngsters grew to enormous proportions. They were finally channeled up the impressive staircase that leads to the doors of the major temple of Christendom.

Wide-awake, gay, noisy, they chatter and even shout. They are barefooted, poorly dressed, but neat and clean. That morning a good scrubbing had been the order of the day. No dirty hands, ragged and torn though their clothes might have been.

Once inside the doors, they start running, racing, anxious to find a place in front of the altar where I am to say Mass for them.

They quiet down as I begin, then their young voices rise to the ceiling of the majestic basilica, while they join together to sing the hymns. Many hundreds of them receive Communion.

I see them there in front of me, as I turn toward them during Mass. Here they are, thousands of small wanderers, in St. Peter's, kneeling in front of an altar. Here are the ragamuffins, the flotsam, the scorned, ridiculed street urchins. These are the beloved little ones of Christ, here they are praying to Him. A part of their joy communicates itself to me and I turn back to the altar shaken and moved.

Mass is over. All of us head for the main staircase leading to the audience chambers. At sight of the Swiss Guards, with their breastplates and casques and halberds, the young visitors are entranced and the Guards find it hard to look impassive under the flood of street-boy comments.

The bronze doors, the gold, the tapestries, the splendor of statues and paintings hold their wide-eyed interest. There is so much to see that the bare feet do not even feel the cold of the marble floors.

"We'll see him . . . the Pope . . . just like the big shots . . . kings, generals, presidents. . . ."

It is the feast day of the *sciuscià*. He is somebody, living, is worth while.

The crowd of children files into the huge Hall of Benediction. His Holiness has wanted to give to this meeting all the dignity and honor of a great audience.

There is a moment of tension, of self-controlled expectation. Small heads, brown and blond and red, curly, smooth, ruffled, are all turned toward a single door, the door through which they know the Pope will come to them.

At his entrance their enthusiasm breaks loose. There is no holding them back. They shout their greetings, they wiggle up the great columns, they balance perilously on the wooden barricade, they stand on the windows, hands outstretched toward the great chair.

"Long live the Pope!"

There is no restraint, no self-consciousness in the cry. It rises spontaneous to their lips. The strangest salutations ever heard come out unrestrained from a thousand throats.

The scene is an unforgettable one. The Pope is as happy

as the children. The kindness of his smile has never been so radiant, as he bends to caress the tousled heads. The children know instinctively they are the favorites in his great flock. "The most dearly beloved," as he himself had said to me a few days before. Poor and tattered as they are, small lost sheep, before him they feel they are as good as anyone else, equals in the sight of God.

At the uplifted hand of the Holy Father, the crowd is quickly quiet.

In the silence, I hear a small *sciuscià* deliver an address, the words at times hardly distinguishable.

The hymn to the Pope, their hymn, rings out from hundreds of throats, maybe a little out of tune, but sung with no reserve of the amount of sound they can produce.

Where could I ever have hoped to assist at such a scene, so charged with feeling and purity of sentiment? For a few moments I speak to the Holy Father and he hands me a very large sum of money for my work.

Silence once again and then the Pope speaks, gives them his blessing, and is gone. But his words will be remembered long through the years:

"Beloved children, we read in your eyes at this moment the joy you feel as you gather here around us. May you read in our own eyes, also, the happiness we feel in greeting you and our gratitude in accepting your gifts, the gift of your prayers and of your hearts that want to be pure and generous.

"Many of you are very small, and all of you are still young, even the oldest. And yet you have experienced life, you have known much misery, great sadness. A few of you may not have had the joy of being born and growing up within the bosom of a God-fearing family. You may not have heard of religion, of priest, of Pope, except to hear them ridiculed and worse. Without knowing it, you may have become accustomed to thinking and speaking in the same way.

"If anyone had ever pointed out the walls of the Vatican to you and told you that some day you would enter there, that we would have been happy to have you here, that you would have been greeted, as by a kind Father who loves you deeply, and that you would have felt at home close to him, full of trust and affection, a few months ago, even, you might not have believed it possible."

The Pope continues. He speaks of the mysteries of faith, of the Babe of Bethlehem born in a stable, as poor as they, of His death on the cross to save them, of the Mother of Christ, the loveliest, the best of all mothers, their mother also, of the mercy and love of an infinite God, ever ready to forgive the small or the big prodigal returning to His Father's house.

"Dearly beloved children," he concludes, "we must leave you now, but our hearts will follow you wherever you are, our prayers will ever be with you, while with deep affection, we impart to you and to those men and women whose kindness hovers over you, whose minds and hearts guide you, Our Apostolic and Fatherly Benediction."

On St. Peter's Square thousands of happy youngsters give vent to their feelings with shouts and songs and laughter and munch away at the lunches prepared for them by the Holy Father's instructions and handed to them as they poured out of the audience hall.

Many of them still linger on the stairs to take a last look at the Swiss Guards and a minor revolution breaks out with first one then scores of inflated paper luncheon bags.

Thus on a gay note is concluded the great audience, and the Guards, who, alarmed at the inexplicable noise, have hurried to the top of the staircase, smile benignly at this show of youthful festivity.

V

TWO WORLDS UNITED IN CHARITY

V

TWO WORLDS UNITED IN CHARITY

> "And the greatest of these is Charity . . ."
>
> Paul

THE CLOSER I DREW TO THESE HOMELESS WAIFS, THE MORE I recognized how really fine they were. Generosity lay deep within their young hearts. To know them was to love them.

God had permitted their heavy crosses, but at the same time He had bestowed upon them the strength with which to cope with and to overcome the hardships of their everyday life. Only this fact could explain why so large a number of them were still basically good and performed acts that might have been called heroic.

But man cannot live alone in the world and children in particular, under the law established by God, must be sustained and helped by those who are older, especially by those who, in the absence of parents, must substitute for them.

In the immediate period after the war, this had been misunderstood or forgotten. The backing and the aid the children needed was not forthcoming. On the other hand, the influences and bad examples met with in lives spent in roaming the streets had been strong and had led them slowly, but surely, astray.

Talking with them, especially with the older ones, I felt that although a longing for better things was still alive in their hearts, their will was being weakened by their disordered existence. More and more urgent became the necessity of saving the younger ones. There we could still hope.

This was not easy, as even the youngest had lost contact with the decent things of life. Their perceptions had been starved, deadened by the constant, demanding struggles for survival. Comprehension, trust, faith were the needed virtues with which to conquer and win them back.

"Get them off the streets!"

This was our oft-repeated cry.

The greatest obstacle with many of them, even greater perhaps than the lack of shelter, was the difficulty of persuading them to enter and live within closed doors. Complete freedom and the unlimited possibilities of acting just as they pleased had made them suspicious of any bait that might hide a curtailment of their privilege of wandering at will. This was especially true of those who most needed this curtailment. It was imperative that a place be found near enough their favorite haunts to persuade them little by little that a change might be to their advantage.

Toward the end of 1945, a young Salesian priest, Father Giorgi, spoke to me of the cellar of a school building where it might be possible to start. Father Giorgi was gifted with that unusual quality that attracts boys, combined with the keen intelligence of the born teacher. The place he suggested was a good choice as it was close to the main station, where it was not hard to find customers for the new venture. It could be the beginning of a stable shelter.

We set to work. Walls were whitewashed, floors scrubbed, showers installed. Bunk beds from our storehouses gave the cellar rooms the appearance of the cabin on a ship. Appropriate frescoes painted by an artist friend added a cheerful note.

The boys began to drift in the first evening, a few at first, more later. Waking up in the morning, they could see the sun rising behind green hills. At night, lying in their bunks, they looked at the moon and counted stars. The sun, the moon, and the stars were only painted on walls and ceiling, but they looked real and very cheerful.

My room, situated near the dormitory, did not boast of any murals, but in compensation my small window looked out on the yard built below street level and, by craning my neck, I could glance up at a tiny patch of sky.

In a short time we had one hundred guests. Little by little they grew accustomed to the daily routine. To some of them, I might even say to all of us, the cellar seemed a paradise.

The very young ones adapted themselves so quickly to the new life that it was a source of amazement to me. In the morning they went to school, taking with them their midday lunch. An older boy accompanied them.

Some of the older boys went to a trade school, others got jobs, while the rest continued for a time at their former varied occupations. Gradually, they as well would fall into line.

I gave the name of Shoeshine Hotel to the new venture, as a kind of guarantee that their just liberty would be respected. There was one rule, however, that had to be obeyed without question and that none of them had great difficulty in accepting. They all had to be home at five-thirty in the evening.

A little before that time most of them would have come clattering down the stone staircase, bubbling over with news of the day's activities. A freshening-up in the bathroom and then down to the business of putting everything in order and preparing for the evening meal. At first it was a cheerful confusion of amateur cooks. Then a group of the older boys was appointed to attend to the kitchen and, after that, woe betide anyone who disturbed the sacred quiet of the "chefs." The younger ones took turns at peeling potatoes, setting the tables, while they looked on in awe at the bosses of the kitchen, who took knowing sips from the big cauldron to taste the "minestrone." Our traditional dish was the *bacalá* — we had been given more than a plentiful supply of this nutritious dried cod — and at first we had *bacalá* undercooked, overcooked, tough, dry, or mushy, each evening until I, myself, developed a marked aversion for cod in any shape or form. Then our cooks gradually improved their style, food became a little more plentiful as the police came round each day with packages of spaghetti, bread, cheese, and other delicacies, confiscated during the raids on the black market. Under this novel diet, cheeks rounded, became rosy. Many of the boys began to look healthy.

Among the more than one hundred boys (they had kept on coming), we had a young French acrobat, the child of circus folk. He had wandered with his father from fair to fair, had slept in the shadow of circus tents, and had idled among the stands where the customers gambled with their money or shot with air guns.

The circus had been an air-raid casualty. His father died. Pierre, an orphan, lived on his own until the Allies took Rome.

We found him one night and took him with us. The smell of *bacalá* was a heavenly aroma to him and the sound of music and singing revived him, both in body and spirit. It reminded him of the old days, under the big top.

Very soon he was entertaining us with the French songs he knew, sung with the alternating brio and languishing air of the real café artiste. He accompanied the words with the language of hands, shoulders, and eloquent dark eyes.

"Sing, Pierre . . ."

Pierre needed little coaxing. He was always the center of a wide circle, the recipient of wild applause, especially when, in the enthusiasm of artistic triumph, he ended his performance with tumbles and cart wheels.

Under the laughter, the scars of old wounds that had not as yet healed were often hidden.

One evening, Saverio, a round-faced, laughing boy, the picture of serenity and happiness, was standing with us in a group.

"What date is tomorrow?" he asked one of the boys.

"The third of February," replied the other.

Saverio's face froze. I happened to be looking at him. He went pale and seemed about to faint. Then he recovered himself.

"Don't you feel well?" I asked.

"I'm fine," he replied.

"What happened to you last night?" I asked him the next day.

He burst into tears.

"My mother died two years ago today."

And so I learned to respect those little worlds hidden in the hearts of each one of them, sanctuaries of sacred memories that could not be touched or spoken of. The boys seemed to have forgotten, but the wounds of loss and the longing for the love and tender care of the years that were gone still remained.

The youngsters of the streets were like tender saplings that had been bent by harsh winds and bitter cold, but the roots had kept strong. It was up to me, to us, to foster and nurture whatever was left of that strength and by understanding and affection bring them back to a normal, useful existence.

At night in the chapel we felt very close, close to God and to one another. The stories of the Gospels, the episodes in the life of Christ never failed to touch in them a feeling of kinship with Our Lord.

Late one evening, a boy was brought in to us by the police. He was fair-haired and delicately featured. Obviously dead with fatigue, he could hardly keep his eyes open. His story was the usual one: home in the Abruzzi destroyed, father and mother dead, a vagabond life, arrival in Rome. His story was so authentically detailed that its very fullness made me suspicious. Then I noticed his oversocks of rough Abruzzi wool and his undeniably mountain boots and I decided that after all there was no reason why his story should not be true. The boys as well were satisfied and they had noses like a fox terrier's for scenting out deception.

One evening, several weeks later, we discovered the truth. He was not an orphan as he had stated and his privations had been of his own choosing. Led by a spirit of adventure, he had run away from home to see exactly how the world was made. We found it out when an automobile drew up at our cellar door. His father stepped out. He had been sent to us after a description of his lost son had reached the Roman police. His son emerged from the kitchen with a potato in one hand and a knife in the other. He was glad to see his father and willingly went home with him. I do not know for certain, but perhaps the memory of the warmth and the cordiality of the boys who had welcomed him in their midst lingered for many a year as a pleasant thought in his mind.

The room I slept in was damp and a period of rain did not improve matters much. I developed a stubborn cough and the doctor gave me the unpleasant news that I had contracted bronchial pneumonia.

To my great disappointment, I had to leave the house, rather the cellar, in the Via Varese and my boys and betake myself to the hospital.

I missed the boys during the month I was away from them and I missed the Salesian Brothers who shared my work each night, when they came to help me after their own day of study was over.

In the doctor's opinion — he was a good friend of mine and did not mince matters — I was the worst patient he had ever had. Whenever he came in unexpectedly, he found my bed and the table near it covered with papers and projects. My recovery was slow. Afterwards, I regarded my sickness as providential, for it had at least given me the opportunity of pondering over the various problems facing me and of making plans for the future.

The best medicine during my sickness was receiving the simple letters and notes sent me by the boys in the Via Varese. Many of them walked daily the three miles that separated us to inquire about me.

As soon as I was allowed to get up, I went to a specialist for an X-ray. His studio happened to be located near the railroad station. While I was inside the house, my car was seen and recognized. No sooner had I stepped out again than I was surrounded by a group of the young *sciuscià* who still plied their trade in the square. I knew them all . . . George with his eyes still sore . . . he had probably neglected to keep up his visits at the eye clinic . . . Andrea, shy and quiet, holding himself in the background. The others made up for his silence. They talked all at once and it was hard to get all they were trying to say. Each one had a piece of news to tell. Giovanni had been picked up by the cops and was in jail. Gino had gone to Milan.

Suddenly one of them pulled out a tiny bunch of flowers they had hurriedly bought and offered it without a word.

"Thank you, son."

Suddenly the world was sunny and misty all at once.

I patted one dark head and jumped into my car.

The crippled children, whom I went to see the next day, greeted me even more effusively. They were being cared for in one of the wings of the Quirinal, the former royal palace.

"We prayed for you every day," said Marco, taking my hand between the two stumps that had been left to him in place of arms and hands.

"Thank you, Marco, you can see the little Jesus you prayed to answered your prayers . . ."

There were so many like him — far too many. And with the maimed and the crippled, there were thousands of little ones who had been blinded. Fifteen thousand mutilated children in Italy alone! What about the thousands in other lands? What about the thousands killed? The millions orphaned? This is war, heroic war that can sound so fine in the pages of a history book or in the news bulletins over the air.

One day the previous summer, I had taken these children into the country on a picnic. They had clung to my hand, they had romped and skipped and shouted their joy at the air, the warm sun, a flower they had held, the song of a bird on the wing.

"Is it pretty, Monsignor?"

Happiness! Joy! An eager face uplifted, lips parted in expectancy . . .

"Very, very pretty, Vittorio."

On Christmas Day they came to my home for a party and a puppet show.

"Listen to Punch . . . he is giving Judy a terrible lecture
. . . wait, the alligator is going to swallow him. . . ."

The blind ones in the audience laughed more uproariously than all the rest. They jumped up and down with
excitement as they heard the stick beating on the poor
wooden head of Punch.

After my convalescence my visits to the mutilated children became fewer and fewer. No longer could I see them
daily. I was living now at my Boys' Town outside of Rome
and only came into the city a couple of times a week. I
wondered what value my short visits could have. Only to
cause tears and mutual regrets at each parting. I would
continue to work for them and beg for them . . . that was
the best thing I could do.

I was wrong. I knew it, when, after three long years, I
went back to visit them with an American friend who had
helped them so much. By now, I thought they would have
forgotten me.

"We have waited for you so long, Monsignor," was the
first thing Vittorio said. He was blind and I had not spoken
to him. I had merely touched his cheek inadvertently as I
used to do years before when he was tiny. "I'm so glad you
have come back!"

They had many things to say.

"Do you remember Gino and the orangeade? Wasn't it
lovely that day? Remember the beating Punch got?"

"They are still talking about that show," the Sister in
charge informed me.

I found them much taller, but they were the same affec-
tionate little fellows I had played with in the meadow. More

tranquil perhaps, a little sadder, with a greater realization of what life meant for them. One of them was so proud of being able to read, his lips running swiftly across the page; another showed his ability in using his artificial hands. Each one was glad of the victory achieved in the battle he had fought so patiently.

"See you again, children. I shall be back soon."

This time I meant every word of it.

My short visits to the numerous houses that sprang up all over Italy brought the same feeling of loss, whenever I had to leave. However, although my work at Santa Marinella, the home for boys near Rome, kept me busy, I did not neglect them. In fact, it was really during this period that saw the beginning of a whole series of new constructions, new children's villages, which I was able to erect thanks to American generosity. All of them had the same aim, the rehabilitation of the homeless and the abandoned. All of them were permanent memories to that sublime sense of brotherhood in the American people.

Among my principal cares was finding a new home for the boys in the Via Varese. They were in good hands, but there was room for improvement as far as the quarters were concerned.

The cellar had been providential when necessity pressed, but it was far from being suitable for a permanent home. The place was small, too small, too dark, with none of the good sunshine and the open spaces for the exercise the boys needed to keep well. It was, moreover, too close to the old haunts where temptation might prove too strong to resist. I kept dreaming of some old building on the outskirts of

Rome, which might possibly be renovated and equipped, but where was it to be found?

The barracks were filled with refugees. Other buildings that might have been useful were occupied by the personnel of the Allied armies, who used them as headquarters and offices. Notwithstanding the interest shown us by highly placed persons, it was impossible to get a suitable place from the Allied Command. Everyone understood and yet everywhere there were other and greater needs, engendered by the state of emergency brought about by the aftermath of the war.

One fine day, the Salesian Fathers informed me that they had found an old fort that had all the appearance of having been abandoned.

I went to see it. The looks of the place certainly did not awaken my unalloyed enthusiasm. The fort was a mere skeleton of a place, ruined by the war and plundered by vagabonds.

The surroundings did hold a certain charm. There were trees and green grass and there were possibilities for the purpose we had in mind. Added to this was the fact that the neighborhood might profit by having a shelter for boys in its midst.

The fort was situated in one of the remote suburbs of Rome. Many families from the capital had migrated there, when the planning of new streets and squares had necessitated their dispossession from their old homes. It was a crowded area and far from progressive.

A fair number of families had clung steadfastly to the tradition of what a home should be. Struck by unemployment, they had nevertheless tried to make a living by fair, honest means. But there were still others who, unnerved by trials and tribulations, had succumbed to the false promises offered by the moment.

Misery and neglect met the onlooker at every turn. Shacks that had been put up temporarily were still standing and crowded. Scores of children played in the mud of the streets. Dust, shattered windows, sagging walls, gray, hopeless people. Their children looked at me and in their eyes was a mute appeal for a better, healthier life.

This time the problems that confronted us seemed unsurmountable and we were almost tempted to give up the project.

We did not. The boys in the Via Varese were waiting and God helped us to fulfill their hopes. One after another the barriers that stood in our path were leveled and we obtained permission to use the old fort.

The Holy Father was our first benefactor. He sent us a substantial contribution and then others came, slowly at first, but at regular intervals. American Relief for Italy, as usual, came to the fore. Construction, renovations began and we were on our way!

The sum received by the A.R.I. at that time and other sums sent later made it possible not only to repair the original buildings, but also to erect new houses with modern equipment.

"May God with the help of His Divine Grace replace the attraction of evil with the appeal of virtue, that idleness and inertia may give way to the joy of honourable work and that the hungry and the naked be given assistance through the

Divine Charity of Christ, the Charity which in a particular manner, must at the present time, take root and grow in the hearts of His followers."

Thus wrote the Holy Father in his encyclical of January 6, 1946. The charity of which he spoke and which I found in the souls of our generous helpers permitted the realization of what, a year before, had seemed a nebulous dream.

On July 18, 1948, in the presence of His Eminence Cardinal Pizzardo, my former chief and one of the greatest of our friends, the new village was formally inaugurated. Present at the celebration were representatives of the new government of Italy and members of the diplomatic corps. In the name of the "Foundation for Homeless Boys," I entrusted the village to the Salesians. On that day was born another of the glorious houses of the Congregation of Don Bosco.

A poet once said that "each tear that is dried on the cheek of a child rises to Heaven as a new-born star." I have no doubt that many a new star found a home on July 18, 1948.

Weeds and refuse had covered this land, the skeleton buildings had lifted impotent arms to heaven. Today the sight that met my eyes was so very different! Gaiety and the fervor of activity were all about me.

The white buildings framed in the green of tall, strong trees held a welcoming look. The sound of happy laughter emerged from those walls, the playing fields were alive with happiness and youth.

Rome from a distance was a tranquil vision of ancient splendor. And yet I knew that inside those antique walls and within the walls of many another Italian city children wept, waiting and hoping that a day might dawn when they, too, would cast off their abandonment and misery.

It was a spring day in 1947 that I landed at La Guardia Field in New York. As foreign representative of A.R.I., Inc., I had come to report on the progress made by the official Italian relief distribution agency in apportioning the immense quantities of relief supplies that A.R.I. had collected and sent to Italy, and to outline Italy's future needs.

The chairman of the board of directors of A.R.I. was Myron Taylor, a good friend of Italy, the President's personal representative to the Vatican and an outstanding benefactor of our street boys.

Judge Marchisio, the president of the A.R.I. was at the airport to meet me. From the start I had admired his generous and self-sacrificing work for war-damaged Italy. He was to become the warmest and most devoted supporter of our work for the boys.

Working with these pre-eminent figures, there had been a host of others, who moved silently, efficiently, coordinating the aid we received, laboring with unselfish fervor to help the unfortunate people of Italy.

I had the good fortune of meeting scores of them, of being a guest in their homes. They were from all walks of life; their homes were often modest, at times poor. I marveled at the warmth of the attachment of the Italo-Americans to the land of their birth. There were representatives of every region of that fair land, but most of

them had come from the southern end of the Peninsula.
After scores of years, the deep-seated love for the country
where they had been born, for the "Old Boot," as they called
it, was still alive. As they talked to me, they went back into
the memoried past, and recalled the field that refused to
yield a fair harvest, the blue bay their fathers returned to at
eve after a hard day's work in the fishing boats, or in the
sulphur mines, where hardships and death were only too
common.

From New York to California, the enthusiasm of everyone for our work was overwhelming. In San Francisco the
press conference lasted an hour and a half. I gave a detailed
account of the work done for the reconstruction of the
country and emphasized the firm determination of the
people of Italy to lift themselves out of the abyss into which
the war had flung them.

This great nation, good, hard-working, thrifty, had the
right to life. It had more than demonstrated by its efforts
during the dramatic period following the war that it possessed the qualities needed to take its place among the
nations standing at the vanguard of civilization.

To feel within us the spirit of Italy is to understand fully
the strength and the forward stride of Western civilization.

The San Francisco reporters showed their amazement at
such enthusiastic words on Italy coming from an Irishman.
They concurred, however, in my judgment that the new
bonds between Italy and the United States should be
strengthened so that the friendship between our two great
people might, in mutual understanding and common aspi-
rations, grow ever stronger.

In Italy often, far too often, we heard of the fabulous
American wealth, and aid was sometimes thought of as
coming only from the rich industrialist or the men who
were predominant in the economic life of the country. In
truth, the help that flowed into the Peninsula from private
individuals more often than not came in offerings made by
the laborer, the mother of a humble home, the farmer,
the man in the street.

As had been the case in Italy, so now in America, I found
that those who had least in the world's goods were the most
generous.

I was invited to speak at a woman's club in a modest
neighborhood in New York City. The mothers and the
wives sitting before me listened attentively as I told them of
the trials the Italian mothers had been asked to bear, of the
superhuman efforts they had made and were making to
save their families.

The meeting over, the women served refreshments and
I stayed on to chat with them. Some of them spoke in a
strange mixture of Italian, English, and the dialect of their
origin. The meaning underlying their words belonged to
only one language, that of the brotherhood of man.

"I should like to do something for the poor 'bambini' of
Italy," said one of them to me, her voice low and shy, "but
the trouble, Monsignor, is that I get paid only once a month
and I'll have to wait until the first. If you are staying in
New York, I'll send you what I can."

She was a hard-working cleaning woman, one of the huge
army that gets busy at night, after everyone else has gone
home, and scrubs, polishes, and dusts the rooms and offices

of the New York skyscrapers. I learned from a friend of hers that each year she was already sending away to a foundling home a large sum for the care and maintenance of two small orphans, in addition to food and clothing.

Face to face with the spirit of such charity, I asked myself who was more blessed, he who gives or the recipient of so much love and devotion?

The universality of this spirit of charity in America gave me food for thought. It was touching that the Italo-Americans should help the land of their ancestors so generously, but much more so when a large number of the contributions came from men and women who were not Italian and had no direct ties with Italy. Add to this that several among them had lost dear ones in the war, sons, brothers, relatives. Their losses had not embittered them. Rather their hearts seemed to have opened wider with a real understanding of the brotherhood of man.

This leveling of frontiers, this consideration of all men as brothers regardless of national boundaries, caused some to fear the wiping out of the love of one's own country. This fear recalled to me Hilaire Belloc's words:

> God gave all men all earth to love
> But since man's heart is small
> Ordained for each one spot should prove
> Beloved over all.

A profound love for our own land should not necessarily prevent that wide comprehension that stretches out toward the whole of humanity. In fact, he who loves his own with a deep, tender affection is likely to feel more strongly the love for his fellow man.

Many committees that were formed in America were the living proof of this particular as well as universal quality that joins together in charity men of different races, origins, languages, traditions, and customs.

How many of my most generous helpers, for instance, most generous not only in money, but in giving of their time, their advice, their unstinted support had been Jews! Their real feeling for our poor children touched me deeply. Nowhere was this better illustrated than in a little incident that happened to me in Philadelphia and that I shall not soon forget.

He was an old man, a Russian Jew, a retired worker on a modest pension and he had entered the room where I was talking to the manager of his union. He sat down on a chair by the door, humbly patient. I asked the official not to keep him waiting and the old man came to the desk.

He took out a handful of dollar bills and coins from his pocket.

"I wanted to send $15 for the children in Italy. Then I heard that Father would be here himself today. I have only $13.50. If you can add the $1.50," he said to the manager, "I will bring it to you next week."

I looked out of the window at the street below. How many of the smartly dressed businessmen, the well-gowned women hastening by, would have bothered to glance at the shabby, bent old man as he walked down the street? Yet, what sublime goodness in him, unsullied by ambition or desire for praise! I felt proud and humbled as I took his hand. If I were ever to waste $15 of the money destined to the children, I would feel that it was these hard-earned, precious dollars I was throwing away!

The committee for the building of the Boys' Village of
Palermo, promoted by the manufacturers, contractors, and
amalgamated clothing workers in the men's clothing industry of New York, was a typical concern made up of men
of Italian origin, but also of many other national groups.

The first time I met with them, I spoke to them of the
plight of the Sicilian children, many of whom were lost and
homeless. If I remember correctly, I also told them the story
of Giuseppe.

Giuseppe was one of the first Sicilian boys I met in
Naples after the fall of the Cassino front. He had no father
or mother. Alone, he had put his few possessions in a knap-
sack and had left Sicily. He was a dark-haired, dark-eyed
boy, his glance loyal, with an undercurrent of deep sadness
in its depths. His independent air, his open smile had
attracted the sympathy of the American soldiers who
adopted him. For a time he lived on the fringes of an army
camp.

The soldiers would willingly have given him food and
clothing, but the natural pride of his race made him despise
begging. He wanted to earn his keep by his own labor, so
in return for his meals and whatever else they might give
him, he offered his services. He was tired at night after
working all day at small jobs, but he was happy. The money
he earned was his and he had kept intact that dignity of
independence that I had seen instinctively defended by
these small outcasts.

After that meeting in Naples, I had not seen him for a long time.

One day I found myself at the station in Rome. The place was crowded with travelers and with boys helping with bags and packages. Suddenly a dark-haired boy popped up beside me.

"Giuseppe, what are you doing here?"

It was really Giuseppe, the small dynamic street boy. Sad to say, he was still a wanderer. He had his shoeshine kit with him and he had been busy getting customers when he spied me.

"I tried to carry the suitcases, but sometimes they were too heavy. I just couldn't make it all day long. Besides, the regular porters don't like us to take their work away from them."

And so Giuseppe had joined the army of the *sciuscià*, not a thief, not an evildoer, but a little man who only wanted to live and be independent of anyone who might lead him astray.

He slept wherever he could, in a doorway or under an archway. I found a family willing to give him food and shelter. After that, I saw him often and I suggested the idea of having him enter a home and live with other boys.

"Oh no, Father, school is not for me."

His way of answering me reminded me of a wild pony rearing in anger at sight of a bridle.

"But you will be with other boys and you will be well treated."

"Sounds like an institution."

"What do you know about institutions? You have never been in one."

"I've never been in one, but a lot of the boys around here have and they ran away."

"Why?"

"Listen, Father . . . just like that, a bell rings . . . no reason, see . . . and then you can't talk . . . you have to walk in single file like soldiers, and then they tell me the food's no good."

"If I opened a boarding school, would you come?"

"Sure . . . why not?"

"But . . ."

"But then it wouldn't be an institution."

I let the conversation drop there. I was not interested in knowing why mine would not be an institution, but his words often came back to me.

Some time later I met a Sicilian friend and his wife. They saw Giuseppe and liked him immediately. He was invited to their home and Giuseppe certainly must have used all his charm, for they adopted him. They had two other sons. They went to school and Giuseppe went also. Why shouldn't he?

"Of course I'm going . . . why not?"

That was Giuseppe.

His life as a *sciuscià* is now a closed chapter. Two, three years go by and I see him again. No more rags. He is tall, serene, but he has not changed. He is still the proud, vibrant boy. His bright soul still shines out of his dark eyes.

Not many of the Sicilian orphans had the same luck.

I visited Palermo again after my return from America. The miserable condition of the poor quarters of the city had not changed. In the hovels around the port, where the air raids had caused so much destruction, the children lived under pitiful conditions. The houses were just mere walls, a roof on top. Not a window, no foundation. The air within was stifling, sour. The lack of sunlight, the wretched food had turned the children into pale, listless wraiths.

I saw them with the bleary eyes of old age, rickety, thin to emaciation. Among the very small, I noticed several with fingers that had been gnawed by rats. Desolation, horror, squalor, lost hope.

Another month went by, but at last, on November 30, 1948, in the presence of representatives of the Italian government, of the highest personalities of Sicily, of the American ambassador and of representatives of the American donors, Boys' Village New York, as it was called, came into being.

The Conca d'Oro (Golden Shell, name given to the plain of Palermo) lies smiling amid shimmering orange groves. The sea's waves do not bite into its beaches and rocks. They touch its shores with a tender caress, they lap softly, almost reverently the ancient land that has seen so many brilliant civilizations. Here Nature has showered beauty with a lavish hand. Even the most unfeeling, the most callous are charmed by the panorama of garden and hill ariot with bloom. Here rises the Palermo Village for Boys.

Near it there are narrow streets and alleyways, such as

are found in monotonous frequency in harbor towns like Genoa, Marseilles, and others, a little more narrow, perhaps less corrupt, but as filled with misery and hunger. From these byways, dreary and wretched, from the miserable huts where no real living can take root because man loves light and air, the boys wend their way to the Village for moral and material good.

It would not be right to attribute all the evils that have weighed down on the homeless children of Italy to the war and its consequences. The scourge and what followed had served to bring to the surface the moral poison of years, to accentuate existing social deficiencies.

The question of the children of convicts has been a problem facing society for centuries. In the literature of the last century, especially in English literature, in Dickens, for example, we can find many a moving passage on the miserable status of these children, who were not orphans and yet were worse off, deprived as they were of home, while father or mother, or both, served time in prison for the commitment of a crime.

Many people have been interested in this social probblem, but often their efforts have been only half-hearted, as though they were doomed to failure, as well as the children.

The good little Calasenctian Sisters in Rome, who had dedicated themselves to the care of these children, had no such fears. Their humble houses were beautiful in the gaiety of their atmosphere and in the affection poured forth on the little ones they sheltered.

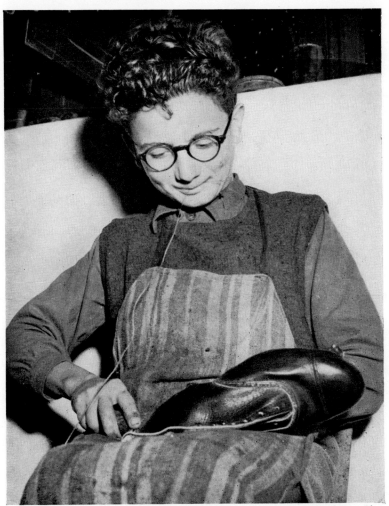

Town Cobbler

Daily town meeting

Recreation rounds out a busy day

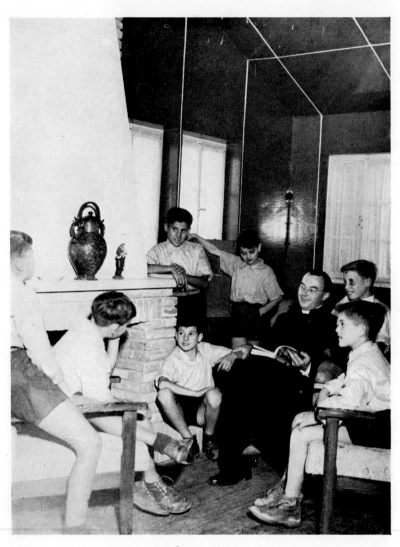

Bedtime Story

Time and again I had marveled at the happiness of the youngsters, the sweetness of their faces, especially when I thought of their sordid background, the bitter experiences in their lives.

The inevitable increase in crime immediately after the war also increased the problems of the little ones: more crimes, more children of criminals. The war and its consequences, the exasperation provoked by sorrow and misery, family tragedies, conjugal infidelity, the unbridled desire for easy gain, the grave deficiencies in the police system — reduced also by Allied orders — caused the explosion of passions with dire results for the protagonists and for the boys and girls who were innocently involved.

The Sisters spoke to me of the necessity of opening a home for these children in Leghorn, the busy seaport reduced to rubble by air bombardments, the Mecca of thousands of vagrant boys attracted there by the colossal deposits of war materiel.

In a few months the home became a reality, an oasis of peace in an old villa on the hills surrounding the port. It was a small place if it were to be compared to the more pretentious ones of the Foundation, but the love found within its walls was the same. The port is a good distance away with its noise and its bustle. The name, Montenero. There is a shrine close by. It is dedicated to the Virgin of Montenero, who watches over her little ones.

Palermo, Rome, Marinella, Leghorn . . . and Pozzuoli. If I go over the road I have traveled, I am forced to note that, more often than not, the spots where Nature has poured its gifts more abundantly, where the sun is warmest, in places dear to the heart of the tourist, there poverty seems to have become more rampant. In compensation, the houses of the Foundation, clean and new, rise close to this poverty, but in the midst of unrivaled panoramas.

Within ten minutes from the center of Naples, other children have found peace and tranquillity and freedom from want.

The view is different from that of Sicily, but the children are the same. They have the same material and spiritual needs, the same reactions, the same feelings.

At Pozzuoli, close to the great port, the Children's Village "Local 48," fruit of the generosity of the members of I.L.G.W.U., is today another dream realized. High on a terraced bluff, it overlooks the sparkling blue waters of the bay.

If the men who were chiefly responsible for it were to return to Italy now, and see the bright cottages in the shade of tall pines, among the fruit trees fragrant with bloom, the little theater, the busy laboratory where the boys are learning to be good tailors, the vast dormitories with windows opened wide on sun-drenched terraces, the glistening showers, the school, and the chapel serene and peaceful, they would have enough recompense for the sacrifices they have made.

Time and the unselfish kindness of good men and women have made the villages grow in number and in usefulness, from the more important ones, such as the "Boys' Citadel" on Monte Mario in Rome, to the smaller, less pretentious ones built with prefabricated cottages. Existing Institutes were enlarged, furnished, improved; recreational centers opened; summer camps inaugurated; sporting fields laid out. More than two hundred thousand children were temporarily helped, more than twenty thousand of them firmly established on the right road and given a chance in life.

In the enumeration of these cold figures, behind each one of which a child in peril is hidden, or a family who may be living in sickness and misery, many, so many facts remain untold.

The work of regeneration did not and when older, wiser, better, the boys left the Institutes and had to face the world again. True, they had grown stronger in resisting temptations, the temptations of old, but they were still asked to face hardships, the hardships of unemployment, of competition, of the search for work that at times cannot be found.

Twenty-year-olds returned to see me, looking for advice, for help, for someone on whom to lean, when all doors seemed shut. Gino, who did not return home at night empty-handed after a day of fruitless search, because "mother is working twice as hard in order to help me," or Adrian, who had been falsely accused of a wrong he knew he had not committed. . . .

More than once have I learned the lesson that even the hardest case cannot and must not be given up. Only patience, unquestioning and indefatigable patience, the patience that bears with and forgives anything and everything, serene in the knowledge that, with the Grace of God, even for these young souls the day of redemption will not be far distant.

VI

THE BOYS' REPUBLIC

VI

THE BOYS' REPUBLIC

"The two corner-stones: Love and Trust"

A WOMAN STOOD WASHING HER CLOTHES AT THE LITTLE fountain facing the main entrance. The crushed sound of each beat, as she lifted and flung each small garment in monotonous repetition against the wooden washboard, mingled with the cries of a child sitting among the refuse on the ground. Other children played around, without vim or vitality. The yard was furrowed by the tires of cars and rutted by the heavier ones of tanks. In the warm June sun, flies and insects enjoyed an undisputed invasion of the place. The broken-down, but still imposing front of the villa, the atmosphere of disorganization around us, the lane of neglected poplars that had led us to the entrance showed the reality to be worse than our expectations.

This was the outside of the villa, which Don Antonio Rivolta and I saw for the first time on June 5, 1945. It was situated on the Via Aurelia, between the small town of Santa Marinella and the port of Civitavecchia. It was in the locality of Tor Marangone, a famous old tower that rises on the coast.

Refugees tenanted the few habitable rooms. In the interior, dusty, blackened by smoke and dirt, with household goods piled in the corners, the walls badly in need of repair, filled with cooking odors, the rudimentary living conditions clearly pointed to the havoc brought about by the war that had just ended.

The bombardments, the occupation by the soldiers of various armies — Italian, German, English, and American — had completely changed the appearance of a gracious summer residence, once so pleasant and hospitable.

There was only one empty room, which had wide holes in the high ceiling. It was a large room, almost sixty feet in length, the windows innocent of glass, the floor of brick, broken and worn. Most of the plaster was on the floor. All in all, it was far from being an ideal place for the boys we had in mind.

What decided us to take it? First, the impossibility of finding another spot closer to Rome. Second, the location of the villa. The nearness to the sea, the open country, the mild climate, the view, gave the place great charm. We could lease it for ten years. In that time we should be able to see how the new center would develop.

The roof was repaired to our satisfaction. The windows were covered with cardboard, burlap, and in a few spots with glass. At one end we placed three rows of double-decker beds and the remaining space was taken up by wooden benches and tables, bandy-legged but still useful. On the outside we built a wash-place and a kitchen protected by a tin roof.

And so, on August 13, 1945, the first boys arrived and barracked themselves in the big hall, which had become dormitory, studio, dining room, recreation room, all rolled

into one. Most of them were the ones whom Don Antonio
had gathered together and met with, a few hours each
week.

In a few months others came from all parts of Italy, some
without homes or family, others I had met with in Rome,
and still others attracted by the news picked up here and
there that a house just for them had been provided. It was
interesting to watch them being absorbed into a democrat-
ically instituted society.

During the first months, the sea, the sunshine, the races
in the fields, the football games with a ball fashioned out
of rags and paper filled the life of the new guests, a varied
and happy existence. Then came November.

The cold winds that at night explored every corner of
the large hall and penetrated the thin blankets, the rain that
by day limited the outdoor games brought not a few discomforts. Still these things were accepted without much
grumbling.

Where grumblings were heard was in the school. There
the boys came in contact with the children of the neighborhood who, though younger than they and not nearly so
smart, could read and write. Most of our boys had never
heard of either and they sensed in this comparison a lowering of their own prestige.

It was tough to have to learn the difference between a
vowel and a consonant, to learn to add, subtract, multiply,
and divide, while sitting down with small "kids" half their
size, but still harder for them was the application of those
lessons meant to teach the elements and the rudimentary
truths of a democratic way of life. The practice of loyalty

rather than of trickery, of honesty not stealth, work in place of idleness, tolerance against violence, liberty without license. These concepts were too ideally ethical for them to value them too quickly, to adapt them without question to their everyday lives.

The winter passed and with it, the cold, the discomforts, the discouragements. The mild spring sunshine chased away the clouds and brought optimism and enthusiasm into their minds and hearts. The end of winter meant also the end of the most critical period in the life of the Village.

That was the winter of my restless days in the hospital, the days in which I planned the kingdom for my boys, a kingdom of peace and friendship. I visioned the dusty roadways as clean straight streets, with small cottages, modern laboratories, public buildings, a real city where the most unfortunate, those who could find support nowhere else, the most difficult characters who were considered hopeless might be able to enjoy the care they needed to grow into a new, healthy existence and be given the opportunity of developing their God-given and so far unsuspected abilities.

My numerous contacts with them had made it possible for me to plumb the depths of these postwar children. I knew all the intimate reasons for their tragic lives. It was then that I began to understand how providential it had been that I had been able to follow, step by step, their long, sad odysseys. It was fortunate that I had met them during air raids, in the miserable, infected caves, in the concentration camps, in the malaria-ravaged districts, in the operating room as the doctor worked on them, in the middle of a street battle, during the period of the liberation, when I had seen from so close at hand the material and moral degeneration taking place in the evil haunts of all the great cities.

Without this personal knowledge of their experiences and their problems, I could never have known the origins of their condition, and thus have been able to understand the varied aspects of their complexities.

I had also listened to the tales told by hundreds of these young vagabonds hounded by the police and by intolerance, the intolerance of small men. They had escaped perils of all kinds, they had been through adventures that bear no telling, they had been exploited and oppressed by unscrupulous adults. Their stories, spun, sometimes seriously, sometimes in jest, often with a naïve attitude toward life, had impressed me deeply and had never been forgotten. Recalling them one by one was useful in helping me to realize what comprehension, will, and tenacity would be needed to wipe clean the black pages in their lives.

It would not be sufficient to give them bread, a bed, clothing, a classroom wherein to gather them for the teaching of a point of grammar, a mathematical problem, or a trade. My heart rebelled against those who think that once these things have been provided they have given their all. The soul does not grow and does not rise, rather it stagnates or becomes deadened if its roots are not watered with the cool spring of understanding and its leaves caressed by the warm sun of brotherly love.

Father Flanagan had fired the imagination of a whole continent by the application of a very simple doctrine: the love of God and its natural consequence, love for your fellow man. Not a cold, strait-laced kind of love, one that fears to show itself and hides ashamed under a resigned exterior, but a glorious outpouring that uses itself without stint to generate confidence, trust, serene comprehension. The two cornerstones of his system (how he would have hated that word): love and trust.

In fact it was not in the application of a new pedagogical method that the reason for the success of his Boys' Town was to be found, but in a philosophy which, banishing all pessimism, discovered in the soul of a child and in his personality inexhaustible resources and possibilities for good.

Love and trust, then, were also to be the cornerstones of the Boys' Town in Italy.

Much was needed to build it. I was not ignorant of the material difficulties that stood in the way of realizing such a project. It was sufficient to cast a glance upon any great institution with its schoolrooms, its trade schools, its theater, gymnasiums, playing fields and add up the cost of each item. It was not a question of having anything superfluous around, but if anything of a serious nature was to be attempted, and the desired results attained, nothing necessary could or should be left out.

Today, when we have almost reached our goal, and in a shorter time than I had hoped for, looking back on the path we trod, I often ask myself whether I would find the courage to walk it again. I think so, for even considering the long, sleepless hours, the delusions, the disappointments, and the battles, through it all I have seen how Divine Providence can make use of our struggles, our inexperience, and our mistakes and turn them into so many instruments working together for the glory of God and the good of humanity.

While Father Antonio Rivolta was busy getting the money together for the purchase of the property, I began my search for the funds that were to be spent in the construction of the Village.

It was natural that I should turn to A.R.I. and to its president, Juvenal Marchisio, for help. Enthusiastically accepting the idea, he gave me his complete and unfailing support and that of his collaborators until the completion of the project.

One of the first gifts I received was a number of prefabricated cottages from the Swiss Wartime Relief, which I had asked for on one of my trips to Switzerland.

"Gee, what luxury!" one of the boys exclaimed when he dashed from the old miserable dormitory into the bright new dwelling.

"Monsignor, those are much too good for us," others said at sight of the new wooden beds.

The night they were to be installed for the first time in their new homes, they did not have to be told to go to bed. After supper, no one was to be seen playing in the garden. Everbody had suddenly disappeared. I found them all stretched out in bed, enjoying the new sensation with the air of gentlemen to the manner born.

"Watch me bounce," one of them called out, as he tested the springs.

"Boy," shouted another, "this is the first real bed I've had in my whole life!"

The boys followed the growth of each new improvement with keen interest, happy at being able to work on the constructions that slowly but surely were beginning to take shape.

After the refugees were all gone, the rooms they vacated were repaired. Then came the small kitchen, more dormitories, the tiny carpenter's shop, a school, and the quarters for the staff. Several people made the remark that it seemed rather boastful to call the place by the name of Village.

"Why call this a village?" asked one visitor with a disparaging air and then with frank candor he added: "I suppose you do it for publicity."

As I had so many times explained to my boys, I told him, also, frankly and with truth, that, in my opinion, a town is not so much made up of the cement and the bricks that had gone into its buildings, as of the citizens it had.

"Some day we shall have the buildings. The citizens we already have."

It was true. The citizens were there, full of life and sincere, for the trust we had placed in them urged them on toward better things. Rough, violent, they slowly began to adapt themselves to the new mode of life. They were encouraged to elect a mayor and he presided daily at the assembly which convened to discuss problems and suggestions.

These problems were carefully considered along with the suggestions, put to a vote, and either approved or rejected. The adults in the Village were allowed to take part and present their views, which were discussed and considered as any of the others.

There was not what is called the authority of the principal, or of a teacher, but the advice of a brother. A brother, whose words were listened to, with open minds and hearts and lacking entirely in any feeling of animosity. In these free discussions, it was possible to follow the line of reasoning of each one and to obtain an ever-growing knowledge of the individual's characteristics. The aim of self-government was, of course, to make the boys themselves their own best collaborators in their growth toward better and greater achievements.

The written law did not yet exist, but it did not take long for the boys to feel the need of it, that their collective living might proceed in a more orderly manner. And the law was written.

The mayor was to be elected by secret ballot. He was then empowered to select his aides: commissioners in charge of finance, public works, education, public health. The assembly ratified the nominations. The commissioners were to see that the individuals carried out certain regulations, and to supervise the working of their own particular departments.

The judge took care of the proper application of the law and any eventual punishment that might have to be applied for its infringement.

The penalties were accepted and carried out in a serious mood. Sometimes it happened that the citizen would resent the humbling of his pride, but somehow he succeeded in keeping away from the football field for a couple of days, or he would patiently wash the restaurant windows, in order to show respect for the law he himself had helped to make. If, however, the defendant thought the imposed penalty unjust, he had the right of appeal at the court of appeals and, if still not satisfied, he could go to the supreme court.

There was a sense of justice, primitive perhaps, even from the beginning, and although the penalties seemed rather strange to the adult mind, they held a value toward building up better characters. It was to be noted, also, that the majority often tried to find every reasonable excuse for a first offender, so as to mitigate the punishment.

"He's only been here a short time and we were just like him and even worse," one would say. "If we give him a hand he'll soon act differently."

And so justice and charity joined hands into a harmonious, astonishing whole, astonishing for us especially who knew from what a world of violence and confusion they had come. A sense of responsibility toward others was slowly developing.

A boy who had arrived at the Village only a short time before approached some picnickers who were eating their lunch on the beach and asked for a piece of cake. He received it. He was heard to say, obviously as a pretext for his request, that at the Village he was not given enough food. A storm of protest broke loose.

He was called before the court.

"Can't you understand that not only did you cut a poor figure, but that you have brought disgrace on all of us?" asked the judge.

"What do I care?" snapped the accused. "I wanted something and I got it . . . that's all that matters to me."

A boy rose to his defense.

"We're free, aren't we? And so if we are, why couldn't he say what he liked to those people?"

The meeting became more and more heated after that. Everyone wanted to have his say, to give his opinion. Finally, the judge called for order.

"Listen, fellows," he said, "do you think that we have the right to speak against our own country to strangers? I don't think so. In fact, we ought not to do it. It's the same thing here. We can speak against the Village, but we shouldn't because it isn't right and it isn't fair."

As he finished, his fists clenched and under the stress of emotion, he burst into tears. Everyone was so stunned and moved by the outburst that not another dissenting word was said.

Talk about reproofs, sermons, and a teacher's admonitions! The words of a boy and his tears held one simple, evident truth: free yes, but free to act the right way, not to follow the wrong.

Freedom of action, but a freedom that never forgot that that of others was another aspect of the same question defined on another occasion.

One of the citizens complained at one of the assembly meetings that for several nights at a stretch he had not been able to sleep, because one of his roommates on coming home made enough noise to awaken the dead.

"So I want to make a noise," shouted the accused as he shot to his feet, "so what? S'posing I want to? Who's go'ne stop me?"

"I ask for the floor," put in one of the members, "you're

right, you are free to make all the noise you like, but Gino is free to sleep when he wants to . . ."

Discussions of points, questions, answers, a proposal, a vote and then came the decision. A new rule had been passed. Silence in the dormitories. No more noise, no more pranks.

In some a feeling for the right was natural, in others it developed slowly, but results were acquiring a positive quality and the hardest characters were gradually becoming docile.

Notwithstanding the fact that the boys seemed more sure of themselves, the security they felt was more apparent than real. The scorn to which they had become accustomed, the hardships they had encountered in their adventurous lives, the lack of personal security during so many years of battle to obtain even the least of their needs had led them to undervalue their possibilities, to lose faith in themselves, to think of themselves as inferior beings.

To accentuate this lack of confidence was added the contact they had with their classmates from the neighborhood who had shown them how great was their ignorance. With the passing of time, some of the old harm was eliminated by the affection and understanding they received, but the roots still remained deep-buried in their hearts. And this came to the fore whenever talks drifted toward a discussion of their future. They still had the impression that they were capable of doing little or nothing that would enable them to live.

I was sitting in the garden one afternoon, sketching some

of the boys playing around me. One of them came to sit on the arm of my chair and watched my pencil as it moved along the paper.

"Do you like to draw?" I asked him.

"How should I know?"

"Want to try?"

"But I'm no good at it."

"How do you know, if you haven't tried?"

He gave in. He took a pencil I handed to him and a sheet of paper and made an attempt at it. He tried his best to put down a nose, a pair of eyes, a mouth. No use. He gave it up and turned to me.

"You see, Father, it looks like nothin' . . . not a man . . . not even like a melon. You see I'm no good . . ."

It had taken only five minutes for him to feel discouraged. But the next day I discovered him in a corner trying his best with pencil and paper. He proudly showed me what he had accomplished, happy at discovering that he was capable of doing something with his own two hands.

This need for self-expression made it urgent that we build laboratories. We had one, the small carpenter's shop, and it was giving a good account of itself. For a long time I had been playing with the idea that it might be possible to put up a laboratory where the boys could learn the art of ceramics. I spoke to a good friend of mine who owned a ceramic factory and he agreed with me that mine was a good idea. With his help the plans were drawn. We obtained the services of an excellent teacher, but what about the money for the building and the equipment?

I cannot lengthen my story too much by giving the details of how a committee of citizens from Baltimore came to our assistance in this new undertaking, otherwise I should have to do the same for all the other American committees that made possible each new cottage, each school building and laboratory, or provided the furnishings and equipment that went into them. It would be a long tale — a tale that some day I shall tell. Here I shall only say that although the fulfillment of this dream cost many sleepless nights, it also brought the joy and satisfaction of making me acquainted with a host of loyal and generous friends, ever ready to share with me the weight of this great responsibility.

The immediate success of the new laboratory encouraged the erection of others. Not so long after, on Industry Square rose a much larger carpentry shop, the machine shop, the mechanics shop and the shoe factory. A space was left for the future building of a printing shop and for other industrial plants. The nucleus of these constructions was the reason for giving the first village the name of Industrial Village, so as to distinguish it from the other two that were beginning to take shape at the same time.

As far back as 1945, I had been faced with one big problem. I realized it would be necessary to give a home to a large number of boys, to justify the construction of workshops and of elementary and professional schools. At the same time I feared that a big increase in the number of our citizens would tend to diminish and finally to destroy that family quality, which is so characteristic of smaller groups. I was furthermore convinced of the utter impossibility of applying the theory of self-government to too large a community.

The solution was reached by building other villages in close proximity to the first. Although the boys of the different villages could use the same schools and central workshops, and benefit by the same medical facilities, they lived their own lives in more autonomous groups.

The first village was well on its way. The time was ripe for thinking of a second one. At first I thought of building it on a hill overlooking the first, but a walk changed my plans.

It was Christmas Day of 1946, a busy day at the Village. Christmas dinner was a joyous occasion. At the head of the table sat the mayor. The conversation, the laughter, the gifts augmented the feeling of peace and happiness as the meal progressed.

The day was a mild one and after dinner we sat in the garden chatting, some of the boys playing at their favorite games. After a while I got up from my seat in the sun and went slowly toward the sea. And there near the old tower, I looked around over the rather neglected wasteland, cluttered with driftwood, and then glanced out to look at the view of sea and island and sky. The cool breeze blew pleasant and refreshing in my face. I stopped short. Why not? Why not a village right here? Why not a Sailors' Village, where boys could play with boats and work with them and become good sailors, while others could fish to their heart's content and grow up fine, healthy fishermen?

I hastened home, sat down at my desk and started to draw, in my mind the vision of new and different cottages and buildings, stronger than the others and able to withstand the salt breezes and the winds that would blow in from the sea as a matter of course on winter nights.

"On the shores of the Tyrrhenian Sea a new, small town will soon rise, feverish with life and activity. And its young citizens, strong in their new-found personalities, will look out toward never-ending horizons, in their hearts the ancient longing to cross the narrow boundaries of their native land, to wander the limitless spaces, where others before them have gone exploring so as to bring honor and glory to their fatherland. . . ."

The words I spoke on the Italian Radio shortly after that memorable Christmas Day proved my enthusiasm for the new project and revealed the fact that I believed in a not too distant realization of it.

"In a year or so," my thoughts had said, but three years were to pass before the new village opened its doors. It had meant new trials and difficulties, but that only made the joy of achievement more complete.

After the Sailors' Village came the turn of the Agricultural Village.

Today the Boys' Republic has come into being. The small, yet great, federation is a growing, living thing. More and more boys come to wander through its streets, along the lanes of luxuriant trees, to live within its walls, its happy cottages, to enjoy its countryside. Life goes on, vibrant and peaceful. It begins anew each day, different, ever-changing.

It begins anew for him who at the sound of the siren hurries toward the factory where the hum of the turner's

lathe awaits him; for him who in the buzz of the electric
saw shapes the wood with steady arm; for the one who
with rhythmic beat drives the nails straight and true into a
leather sole; for the one in the field, no longer in fear of
the patient ox. They live in their own city, in a republic
that belongs to them, a republic to which they have given
a soul, a life, and a law. They know its every corner . . .
so many among them have seen it born and grow strong!
And tomorrow and for many tomorrows they will speak of
it proudly to their friends and their families. Perhaps they
will describe it in words such as these:

"You went in through a tall gate which was always open,
because any homeless boy could enter, for he knew in
the Republic all were made welcome. A lane of trees led
to the center of the town, to Pius XII Square with its lovely
old buildings, its high pillars. There was the restaurant
with frescoes on its walls! These told the story of ancient
maritime republics. Down at the end was the one we liked
best. It was of our own Republic and its coat-of-arms: a
caravel riding the seas, its full sails swelling to the breeze.
There was a little church and its painting of the Madonna,
the Madonna of the Homeless Boy. And flowers, flowers
everywhere, climbing up the walls, circling the assembly
hall, flowers around Monsignor's tiny house where we went
whenever we felt like it, for the door was always open and
we knew he would be glad to see us, to talk with us.

"We liked everything about the place. Everything was
so beautiful especially at night when the moon almost put
out the light of the street lamps. Then it was pleasant to
take a walk to the beach and to the Sailors' Village, where

the boats were at rest in the port and the peace of the night was broken only by the song of a boy.

> I want to go to America,
> but it is so far away . . .

"Sometimes we wandered up the country lane that led to the Agricultural Village with its wide roofs and the arches of its porticoes reminding you of an Alpine village. Here also the same peace, the same life, the same brotherhood in joy as well as in pain."

I have said that each day brings new life into the Republic, different and harmonious. Varied, as in every great city or small town of the world, for there, as elsewhere, men are growing, little men who have already tasted of the bitterness of life.

There is singing to be heard as the turner's wheel hums. The slender vase takes shape in smooth curves, polished, gleaming under the skillful fingers obeying the young mind that guides them.

"Look at it rise!" calls out the turner to his friend.

He is as happy as the little fellow who looks at the tiny statues he has fashioned, a peasant, a small donkey, an ox born of his delicate, tapering hand. As proud as his companion, busy decorating a plate with leaves and scrolls of renaissance color and taste.

Each one tries to outdo the other, to do better in friendly rivalry, the gardener at his flower bed, or the young farmer in the field, as they proudly point out their work.

"Monsignor, look at the flowers I got! Look at them! And to think I planted them all by myself! Gee!"

"My lettuce is coming along fine . . . now, in go the tomatoes!"

These are the younger ones, under the expert guidance of a master farmer and equipped with the smallest of tools for digging and sowing and planting.

"Hey there, don't step on that bed . . . want to spoil everything? Took me a month to get that far. . . ."

Yes, it was also an ever-changing life. It changed when summer meant camp life, walks in the woods and in the hills and mountains, swims in the cool waters of the sea, campfires in the evening, sunshine, starlight, moonlight. Spring brought its flowers, winter its nights sitting round the fire, music on the radio, stories told and games and songs.

Style enters in at the Republic. One day the style starts with a pair of skates and for a time everyone skates wildly through streets and squares. Then someone gets two small wheels and fashions himself a scooter. After that it's a race to see who will build the next one. Divided into teams, they search wildly in the hills for hidden treasures. They need air and motion and so return with new strength and vigor to their work.

Football games, basketball, races, anything. . . .

On the great feast days, in which the boys participate with moving candor and openness of soul, an unusually lively atmosphere pervades the square. The citizens, smart in their best clothes, stand around in groups and chat, as is the custom in every town square of the world.

The band swings by and breaks the air with gay compelling melodies while the crowds applaud. Music! It is the great passion of many and a visitor may stand amazed to hear the notes of Tschaikowsky and Dukas whistled melodiously and with soft inflection as a boy strolls by.

There is a piano in my cottage and when I play the silence is immediate. Even the sports news on the radio is turned down.

It is a favorite spot in the evening, that cottage. If it is winter, to sit around the fire and listen to old tales and recount the new, more tragic fables of their own. If I am at my desk, the questions cannot be numbered.

"Have you read all of these books? What is the highest mountain in the world? In America, did you see President Truman?"

In the silence of early night, the church bell is ringing for evening meditation. Few are missing. It is perhaps the most intimate moment of the day. The boys pray . . . for the mother who is dead . . . for "Johnny" who is sick at the hospital . . . for the homeless boys of the whole world . . . and they mean their prayers. The word "brotherhood" seems to have gained a newer, higher meaning.

I speak to them simply and briefly:

"When in life suffering touches us, let us see in it a proof of God's special trust and love for us. On the field of battle, the officer calls out one of his men and sends him on a dangerous mission, perhaps to his death. The soldier is proud of this trust, he needs not be told again to do his duty. He knows his duty and he follows on and does it, not counting the cost. God chooses His own among the men of the world and to them He gives, entrusts a mission, that of suffering with Him, that others may gain life through them, everlasting life. They can refuse, if they wish to have a life of greater ease and security. We will not refuse, we of the Republic, we will not even ask Him the reason for His will, for by now we are convinced that through suffering alone, shall we come into a fuller, a more perfect life. In such an acceptance, we shall be able to give unto others the highest proof of the depths and the force of love."

My audience understands my words. Their eyes, clear and serene and unafraid, look at me. They are the children of the war who through horror, pain, and sorrow have awakened to love.

EPILOGUE

EPILOGUE

"... that proud and strong and free, they may live again ..."

THE CITIZENS OF THE BOYS' REPUBLIC HAVE FOUND THEIR place, their way in the world. It is up to them to follow it well. But what about the others? My thoughts turn back to the first pages of this book, to the lines of ghostly figures, the lost children of the world.

Figures no longer matter, nor the piles of paper used, the many telephone calls made, the many journeys taken throughout Europe, America, the world ... and art, music, and the beauties of Nature no longer soothe my spirit. Nor the vision of magnificent buildings, huge piles of stone upon stone. For, for the homeless ones, there is no word of consolation, and we do not seem able to find all of these children who walk along the great highways of the world, turning the corners of gigantic buildings, children who huddle cold and shivering under the approaches of majestic bridges, that spring outward across rivers, boys who stroll aimlessly yet hopeful through the sumptuous gardens of our big cities. We are not able to make out all those specters who wander with heavy feet and heavier hearts through the fogs of London, under the hot sun of Sicily, in the stone canyons of Manhattan, and on the wide sidewalks of Rio de Janeiro. We have not yet had the good fortune of seeing them smile. Even as then, they have no faces.

But we must know, we want to know who they are. We want to point them out one by one, to fight for the rights of each one of them, that their smiles may rise spontaneous, that their ghosts may take shape, that proud and strong and free, they may live again and walk with us side by side on the road that has no ending.